Just Add Blood offers an extraordinarily insightful and profound understanding of the value of runelore to the modern mind. Combining esoteric and psychological understanding, Kennan Taylor has succeeded in revealing the ways in which our lives today can be enriched with this ancient system.
Philip Carr-Gomm, Chief of the Order of Bards Ovates & Druids. Author of *Sacred Places* and co-author of *The Book of English Magic*

Dr Kennan Taylor has provided a valuable, novel and insightful contribution to the field of runelore; in particular, the Anglo-Saxon runes.

With my knowledge of Dr Taylor's work and interest in this field, I anticipate *Just Add Blood* to be the forerunner of other more detailed works in this field and the associated ones of magic and neo-pagan spirituality.

I also appreciate that it will both support and develop Dr Taylor's online presence, and the commitment he has in furthering this from a therapeutic and educational perspective.
Dr Ian Cook, Politics and International Studies, School of Social Sciences and Humanities, Murdoch University, Western Australia

Just Add Blood offers the kind of historical and cultural depth which is often missing from publications concerning runes or other divination or oracular systems. It is a work in progress, but it shows strong promise of rendering the symbolic referents and cultural contexts for the use of the runes in such a way that the material will be of great relevance to those who wish to explore the divinatory and spiritual development domains.

The work will benefit from additional, carefully structured treatments of the cultural histories of rune systems and detailed frameworks for use of the material in a practical sense.

Dr. Taylor has the requisite skill, intellectually, creatively and in terms of writing skills to produce a publication of some considerable value. It would certainly be of interest to readers with backgrounds in esoteric theory and practice, shamanism and anthropology.

Rafael G. Locke, National Director, Spirit of the Earth Medicine Society, Australia. National Director, Ikon International Institute, Australia. Visiting Professor, Department of Psychiatry and Neurobehavioural Sciences, University of Virginia, Charlottesville, VA, USA

Just Add Blood is a welcome addition to the world of spirituality and its mysteries. Kennan Taylor has brought his expression of Runelore from out of the mists into the open as a gift for the use of existing and emerging practitioners, and new seekers of the seemingly lost soul. Kennan's psycho-spiritual approach to the world is evident as he takes the reader on a journey into the world of Runelore.

Metaphysically, blood is the song of the soul and has magical qualities. It transforms the individual as it travels through veins and eventually sings in the heart. As a Keeper of the Stones and thus a practitioner of ancient ways I was hugely impressed by Kennan's interpretation of the Runes, an ancient form of divination directly imparted from the Gods. To hold a Rune in one's hand is to take the blood of the Gods into oneself.

Given that humanity has shifted a notch upwards in its search for a deeper consciousness the Runes offer an avenue into the world of the new occultist and emerging mystic. The Runes provide a bridge from the mundane to the world of spirit, an entry into a level of consciousness, where there is direct contact with the vital force that sings, more often than not, unheard, within each of us.

Casting a Rune, either singly or in a spread, evokes a response from the world of spirit and, as Kennan states, re-establishes a connection, a relationship, to the greater reality in which we are embedded. Once that connection is made, there is no going back, only going forward into a greater understanding. It is the beginning and, for many, all it takes is to hold a Rune.

Anni Hoddinott, Metaphysical Priest; Keeper of the Stones & Medicine Ways

Just Add Blood is a captivating work, leading us gently, but swiftly and assuredly into the worlds and realms of Runelore.

As a guide, teacher, mentor and most importantly, fellow traveller, Kennan Taylor lays before the reader this ancient domain of mystery and magic and explains it in ways which are meaningful, intelligent, relevant and indeed vital; as an agent with potent possibilities for the "recovery of individual and communal soulfulness" in our contemporary times.

More than scholarly, this work brings to its subject matter, the authenticity of the lived experience of the human condition and its search for meaning, across the span of history to the present day.

To bring forward the ancient pillars of wisdom of the past, fully and authentically to the present and then to enable fellow human beings to rise and stand upon them, to look to their future confidently; informed and connected to that which is greater than themselves, is no mean feat ... and in this, Kennan has succeeded with brilliance and integrity! ...

A competent, alchemic synthesis of history, culture, heritage, landscape, mystery and imagination ... true medicine for our times!

Stuart McDonough, Clinical Nurse Specialist (Mental Health)

Just Add Blood

Runelore: Understanding and Using
the Anglo-Saxon Runes

MOON
BOOKS

Winchester, UK
Washington, USA

Just Add Blood

Runelore: Understanding and Using the Anglo-Saxon Runes

Dr Kennan Taylor

MOON
BOOKS

Winchester, UK
Washington, USA

First published by Moon Books, 2014
Moon Books is an imprint of John Hunt Publishing Ltd., Laurel House, Station Approach,
Alresford, Hants, SO24 9JH, UK
office1@jhpbooks.net
www.johnhuntpublishing.com
www.moon-books.net

For distributor details and how to order please visit the 'Ordering' section on our website.

Text copyright: Dr Kennan Taylor 2013

ISBN: 978 1 78279 401 1

A CIP catalogue record for this book is available from the British Library.

Design: Lee Nash

Printed and bound by CPI Group (UK) Ltd, Croydon, CR0 4YY

We operate a distinctive and ethical publishing philosophy in all
areas of our business, from our global network of authors to
production and worldwide distribution.

CONTENTS

Preface

Just Add Blood is an introduction to a personal study and use of the Anglo-Saxon runes. This small book will serve both as a point of reference, and also as a guide in how to use the runes. Inevitably, this will have my own personal imprimatur in a vast, expanding, and often confusing field. As I anticipate more research and writing about runes, extending to my interest in Anglo-Saxon (or Old English) medicine, magic, and spirituality, I have entitled the whole field – as some other commentators have – Runelore.

To begin, a few words about the content. If you are eager, then the short introduction will give you sufficient background before progressing to the 'how to use the runes' section; how much of this you want to read will depend on your prior experience with runes, divination, and magic. The extended introduction is to give a more detailed context for the runes, to illuminate what has been called the 'Dark Ages', and to reveal that they were far from dark; indeed, an appreciation of this period gives a more grounded and traditional context for the modern age and its attendant challenges and dilemmas.

Then we move into the Anglo-Saxon Futhorc, in two stages, so as to provide continuity with the Germanic or Teutonic Traditions; but also to differentiate the differences, and the progression of Anglo-Saxon magic and spirituality within this period. The postscript hopefully fills in any lingering gaps, whilst the appendices provide the background and detail referred to, but not included in, the main text. A short bibliography follows, so that if you are relatively new to runelore you may start a more extended research. Most of these books will then provide bibliographies so that you can pursue your areas of interest further.

Just Add Blood has an acronym – JAB – that may amuse you. It was an inspirational idea that serves to highlight what I believe is a significant focus of runelore; that is, the role of magic and sacrifice.

Symbolically blood is a very powerful vital fluid. In our day and age blood carries a significance that is almost fearful, as we associate it with a variety of diseases; yet it can be life saving, as with transfusions. Blood is a symbol of power, as indicated in the sacrifice of many forms of execution. Yet at a deeper spiritual level it is representative of the power of death and transformation, as in the blood of the Eucharist. Drawing and using one's own blood is not only a powerful act, but it is also a magical act and should be approached – and used – with caution; as well as with the support of ritual and within a spiritual context.

It is relatively obvious to me that runes emerge from prehistory, within whatever priestly caste defined the time, as a tool of communication with the gods or – in modern terminology – the transpersonal or archetypal forces that shape, define, and govern our existence. It is no surprise, therefore, that as language and writing emerged for more routine, mundane, and profane means of communication, that runes took an occult and separate pathway into a more esoteric system of communication. They have maintained this position, and it is a source of profound interest to me that they have re-emerged in an age that is decidedly godless.

This means of communication required and still requires various modes, such as appropriate time, location, ritual, and varying degrees of altered states of consciousness. However, such an orientation usually and necessarily demands a level of sacrifice. In the context here, *Just Add Blood* indicates that the sacrifice was – and is – fundamentally that: the use of the practitioner's own blood from a sacrificial wound that is embedded in the runes, which are usually carved or engraved onto wooden or stone staves.

Overall my orientation can be mapped on a cross that is like a compass. I try to balance the east of academia with the west of esoteric speculation, and the south of our traditional past with the north of the future. As may become apparent in the book, I see my place in the west of Australia as a modern equivalent to or even metaphor of the migration of the Anglo-Saxon peoples and their spirituality, as well as a furtherance of the Runic Tradition. In this respect I believe Australasia has much to offer the future of the planet we call home.

Brief Introduction

Historically the runes stem from the Teutonic regions, considered as mainly modern-day Germany, early in the Common Era (CE); although some commentators would see their origins to be many centuries earlier. In fact, the runes may represent an unbroken tradition from the Stone Age, as cave drawings and other preserved objects have painted and etched symbols with a runic quality. If so, they arise with the dawn of human consciousness and its evolution, representing an ancient means of communication.

By the time the runes emerged historically, the Celts, also a Teutonic people, had migrated to Britain (500 before the Common Era, or BCE) and developed their own culture there, with input from the indigenous peoples they superseded. At the start of the Common Era (CE) the Celts themselves were superseded by the Romans, in much of what is now present-day England.

Meanwhile, within Germany, many tribes were preparing to migrate and expand their influence. So, after the Roman departure in the 5th century CE the vacuum in England was filled by Angles, Saxons, and Jutes, collectively referred to as the Anglo-Saxons. They brought the early runes with them, which at this time had settled into an 'alphabet' of sorts. This rune row, or the linear sequence of runes, was called the Elder Futhark and comprised 24 runes, so named after the first six runes ('th' is one rune).

The Anglo-Saxons were relatively confined to England and evolved into what we know now as the English race. Ireland, Wales and the west of England remained more Celtic, as did Scotland with the Picts and Scots. This should be considered a very fluid state of affairs; although our interest is marked by runic finds, which tend to be almost exclusively in the regions occupied by the Anglo-Saxons.

In these so-called Dark Ages the runes took on a distinctly English character and extra runes were added to the Elder Futhark's 24 runes. These extra runes number between 4 and 5. Around the 8th and 9th centuries a further expansion of the Futhorc occurred in Northumbria so that there were now 33 runes in total. Also with a change of the 4th and 6th runes in name, shape, and phonetic expression, the Elder Futhark became in time the Anglo-Saxon or Old English Futhorc.

Over this same period the Anglo-Saxon language developed and adopted the Roman script to become Old English. Although the runes have phonetic values that could be used for writing, this did not generally occur, except as inscriptions. This may be due to the fact that the runes always had a magical component, so were increasingly and more exclusively used in this way; whereas the Roman script under Christianisation, lacking this dimension, became more suitable and available for everyday usage.

This more magical association of the runes is detected in the later runes of the completed Futhorc. It is also apparent in the Viking era between 800 CE and 1100 CE when, in northern Germany and Scandinavia, the rune row of the Elder Futhark underwent a reduction to 16 runes and being subsequently known as the Younger Futhark. This may have been an attempt to re-establish the more magical use of the runes in the face of the progressive Christianisation that was occurring during this period. With the completion of Christianisation in Scandinavia the Viking era came to a close around 1100 CE.

In Britain, Christianisation had been a lot earlier, properly beginning in the 7th century, although present before then. Christianity provided a significant cultural influence, but seemingly ignored the runes (perhaps due to denial, repression, exorcism, or all of those things), with the exception of the Northumbrian input. Influences from the Celtic era may be seen in the 4 to 5 runes that developed immediately after colonisation, as trees are strongly present. It is thought that the Celts and their priesthood, the Druids, used a magical system called Ogham that was based on trees.

After the close of the Viking era, runes and the various Futharks (a collective term comprising all three rune rows) disappeared from public view. However, this was not true of traditions within these now Christian cultures that held to the 'old ways', and also in the folk traditions there. Obviously the runes never completely died out, making occasional appearances, until the increasing interest and re-emergence over the last few centuries.

We know of the runes through archaeological finds. These are on ornaments, coins, stones, and in manuscripts. They were probably more commonly and magically used on materials that could be sacrificed and would not have survived anyway, such as wood. Collectively these give us the rough outlines that have fleshed out all of the Futharks. But there is collateral evidence regarding runes that extends to their meanings and, although being handed down from Christian scribes, there exists what are known as rune poems.

The Old English rune poem of the 8th or 9th century survived in its original manuscript form until being destroyed in a fire in the 18th century. Luckily a copy was made some years prior, with the additional inscription and assignment of actual runes to each of the 29 poems. Although a later interpolation, there is good evidence to support its validity and the associations are generally accepted in the academic community.

In the Viking era the rune poems of the Younger Futhark were written down in two versions, firstly the Icelandic version in the 13th century, with the Nordic following a couple of centuries later. Again these were by a Christian hand, but they serve to corroborate the Old English poem, even though the poems (or riddles) themselves are often quite different in context. Unfortunately there is no equivalent rune poem for the Elder Futhark.

We now have several levels of potential meaning in the runes. There is the pictorial representation that is itself symbolic. Assisted by the mixture of Roman and runic scripts over time we also have a definite phonetic sequence, as well as names for each rune, themselves of symbolic significance. The rune poems add another level of meaning, often in what could traditionally be seen as riddles or charms.

Indeed, a poem sourced in the Icelandic Poetic Edda of the Viking era, called the Havamal, describes the god Odin (Woden in Old English) obtaining the runes by an act of self-sacrifice, where he also utters eighteen charms associated with them. The significance here, as the charms do not readily correlate with specific runes, is the relationship of Teutonic mythology to runology. Additionally, Odin's act is sacrificial in a manner not dissimilar to Christ on the cross, and which we would now call shamanic.

There is much more evidence available than in this simplified version, quite obviously, but nothing that contravenes this brief outline. In fact, the whole academic and scholarly field is awaiting further finds to fill in the gaps and to adjust our thinking on the subject.

In the modern era we have rediscovered the runes and are also rediscovering their significance, but is this just a historical accident? I think not. I consider it may be what is known as the 'return of the repressed' on a collective level. With the decline of Christianity as a spiritual influence and the waning of the Church's political and cultural control, the runes are resurfacing with other cultural reconnections (of which the New Age is replete, in content if not always in accuracy).

Many of us have an Anglo-Saxon heritage. If that is the case then it is most likely that spiritual traditions from your heritage and their more magical tools will strike an internal resonance. This is primarily emotional and a feature of anything returning from a personally repressed position, although this emotional feeling is deeper and more psycho-spiritual if it is collective and from our heritage.

In the modern era we have also focussed a lot on the Elder Futhark, and this has greatly facilitated this rediscovery process. However, there is the extant and distinctly Anglo-Saxon rune row that has not, in my opinion, been fully explored. That is why I am using the Futhorc exclusively here; though not without reference to the other two Futharks, their significance, and the traditions they came from.

Within the Christian tradition the concept of 'soul' has become marginalised, although this term is in dire need of restoration, as many moderns are looking for a more 'direct' spiritual connection. In a sense this is where the more esoteric traditions within established religious structures are resurfacing, as well as those from other traditions. We are familiar with such eastern influences; it is time to look in our own backyard.

To my mind the runes fulfil this function for many. The soul is asking firstly for her own voice, and secondly for a path back to the divine. In less mystical terms this is establishing a relationship with the greater reality that pervades and permeates our very existence. This relationship has a language that is necessarily symbolic and imaginative. Not only do the runes fulfil this criterion, it may be that the 'greater reality' itself is using them as a means for getting back in contact with its 'lost children'.

Poetic and spiritual metaphors notwithstanding, the runes are a magical system par excellence. They are rich in meaning, challenging to work with, and make a demand on our morals asking us to fulfil our individual fate, or what the Teutonic peoples refer to as 'wyrd'.

Extended Introduction

In modern times runes are considered within the realms of magic and divination. Indeed the word rune itself can mean a 'secret', 'mystery', or even a 'whisper'. There are differing levels of understanding or 'kenning' condensed here: spelling as writing and 'spells' as magic, secrets as things hidden and mystery as things unknown yet also unknowable. These different levels pervade our reality, although in modern times there is a tendency to collapse the unknown and unknowable into the known, to reduce the symbolic to the literal and the magical to the scientific.

My belief is that one significant aspect of the modern attraction to runes is the reconnection with and restoration of this greater mysterious and spiritual reality. Indeed, it could be argued that this reality itself is making itself known through means such as the runes; providing a direct access for us to the 'gods', and not through the often redundant or closed channels of established religion. It may be that we lose our traditional background and ancestral heritage at our peril, and that one function of runelore is to reverse this process and restore a more holistic harmony. Essentially I see runelore as a tradition that is integral to human consciousness and its evolution.

It was stated in the earlier brief introduction, but is worth reiterating, that within psycho-spiritual terminology the soul is primarily asking for her own voice, and secondly for a path back to the divine. In less mystical terms this translates to establishing a relationship with the greater reality that pervades and permeates our mundane existence, be that God or the gods. This relationship has a language that is necessarily metaphoric, symbolic, and imaginative. Not only do the runes fulfil this criterion, it may be that this 'greater reality' itself is using them as a means for getting back in contact with its 'lost children'.

The actual source of the runes is undetermined, although they are primarily and ultimately associated with the Teutonic races, which includes modern England, Germany, Holland, Scandinavia, and East Germany – formerly the Goths. The last is now historical, but my personal and intuitive impression is that the Gothic contribution to the runic corpus has not been fully considered. Greek influences may flow through the Gothic channels; the Latin influence appears relatively obvious with some runes, but does not extend to the whole corpus, which probably predates Latin itself. Etruscan (northern Italian) as source material is the currently favoured academic option and is well supported with evidence, although the reverse – that runes may be source material in their own right – is not generally considered.

Part of the confusion surrounds the fact that we are so accustomed to the modern alphabet, that we do not fully appreciate that there are scripts where the 'letters' also have an inherent and esoteric meaning. So, when the runic script is explored from this 'literal' perspective only, it will necessarily be incomplete. The Etruscan, Roman, and Greek scripts do not have letters with an associated word 'meaning'. For example, the Elder Futhark runic letter 'f' also has the name **Fehu**, which means cattle, value, or fee; but the Roman equivalent does not have a similar extension. So, whilst some Roman letters may have been imported into the runic script, the actual meanings would have been either indigenous to the Germanic peoples or gained from elsewhere. Maybe a lot of this confusion awaits further evidence and discoveries, because from a scholarly perspective the field seems to have been well tilled to date.

There is considerable debate about the time of origin of the runes. The two first centuries of the Common Era (CE) are supported by archaeological evidence and considered the recognised historical minimum. Although, because of the nature of some materials used (wood etc., which would be either naturally or sacrificially destroyed) for which there is no record, an earlier time is widely speculated, even to several hundred years before the Common Era (BCE). Older epigraphic evidence starts to merge with other forms of pictographic expression as we move backwards in time beyond the Common Era. So the 'reverse' view – that the runes emerged from a proto-language and symbolic system that parallels human evolution – is the most likely scenario and would represent a rich source of enquiry.

In the period of the early centuries of the CE the generally held view is that there existed what is now called the Elder Futhark, consisting of 24 runes, which is the basis of study for all practical purposes: it is this that most commentators refer to. The term Futhark is derived from the first six runes ('th' represents one rune, **Thurisaz**) that are common to all rune systems.

This Elder Futhark was then used in England after some of the Germanic races (the Angles, Saxons, and Jutes – hereafter referred to collectively as 'Anglo-Saxon') migrated to the south and east of England after the Roman departure early in the 5th century of the CE; although contact, particularly in the north with Scandinavia, would have long been in existence and also less under Roman influence. With the Viking expansion of the 9th century the occupation of much of England in the north and east (Northumbria and East Anglia) was under their direct control (the so-called 'Danelaw'), leaving only Wessex and parts of Mercia as distinctly Anglo-Saxon.

During this period the runes underwent some phonetic modification and a progressive extension, with the 4th or 'a' rune becoming an 'o', and a (hard) 'c' used instead of the 'k' of the 6th rune, such that this Anglo-Saxon system became referred to as the Anglo-Saxon or Old English Futhorc. Note the spelling change of 'Futhark' to 'Futhorc' as a consequence, sometimes via a transitional 'Futhork', which is still occasionally used. As well as some other modifications to rune shapes, names, and sounds, there were some additional runes added in England such that the

Futhorc numbers anywhere between the original 24 and 33 runes. The extension is commonly to 28 or 29 (as in the Old English rune poem), with the last four added later and being peculiar to Northumbria.

In Scandinavia the Elder Futhark underwent a radical revision and reduction during the Viking era (800 CE – 1100 CE) from 24 to 16 runes, and it subsequently became referred to as the Younger Futhark. The reasons for this are unclear, but mark a possible division between magico-religious purposes and the usage of runes as a simple script, as well as an attempt to re-establish a more traditional religious autonomy in the face of advancing Christianity.

The Roman script ultimately predominated during this entire period (400 CE – 1100 CE) and this was contemporaneous with the Christianisation of Northern Europe. This process was progressively northwards and completed in Iceland by the end of the millennium, although somewhat later in some parts of Scandinavia. Of interest in this process is that Iceland was the only country to achieve conversion democratically.

The runes then relatively disappear from public view after the Norman invasion of England in 1066 and the close of the Viking era around 1100, with sporadic appearances over the second millennium, culminating in the modern 'revival' of interest in runelore. It should not be forgotten that the Normans, although from France, were originally 'Norsemen' from Scandinavia.

Common materials for carving runes on or in are wood (there are many and frequent references to trees in all of the Futharks), bone (possibly ritualistic), coins (generally from the middle of the first millennium), epigraphic use on stones, and in manuscripts. Whilst stone runes occur predominantly in Scandinavia, interestingly there is a cluster in northern rather than southern England, often in religious settings and possibly reflecting the ongoing Norse and Viking influences.

Other sources of information include the rune poems. The Old

English rune poem dates from the 8th or 9th century, written by Christian scribes from earlier oral sources. (A fire destroyed the original in the 18th century, but an earlier accurate copy exists.) This poem describes 29 runes. The Scandinavian Younger Futhark is referred to in two poems recorded in the 13th (Norway) and 15th centuries (Iceland), also in Christian sources. There is, unfortunately, no equivalent poem for the Elder Futhark and so the English rune poem is often referred to for understanding the Elder Futhark, although modified by the Scandinavian rune poems (but obviously this is only possible for 16 of the 24 runes); an attempt maybe, by some commentators, to gain a clearer or more 'original and authentic' meaning from the Teutonic perspective, as there are significant differences in the poems.

These are the basic facts, but what are the varied reasons that stand behind them? Here we meet a mixture of knowledge, opinion, and speculation over a very wide spectrum.

The more academic and scholarly position (e.g. RI Page, particularly with regard to the English Futhorc) is generally literal and mundane, and posits that runes represent a script for various purposes, such as communication, legal documents, possession of property, and epigraphs. It eschews a primarily religious or magical dimension, and indeed the evidence as such does not overtly and directly support one.

Yet the circumstantial evidence seems overwhelming, together with the fact that the modern alphabet and runic scripts appear side-by-side in many finds, indicating that the latter were used for a fundamentally different purpose. However, as with other disciplines – modern western medicine, for example – a strict scientific and evidence-based methodology does not include more speculative and intuitive approaches, and would also tend to deny the existence of a magico-religious influence by exclusion, repression, and literalisation.

Here is where I part company with the strict scholarly

approach. I am not alone in this: RWV Elliott retains a sound scholarly background in the Futhorc, yet does cross the divide into the magico-religious. Edred Thorsson has a PhD in this academic domain and yet champions a modern Germanic magico-religious view around runology and the Futhark. Others have followed Thorsson (e.g. Kveldulf Gundarsson) in the Germanic domain (both are from a North American background). The varied input of JRR Tolkien has, in my opinion, yet to be thoroughly assessed.

Interestingly, the Anglo-Saxon Futhorc gets a more psycho-social orientation (e.g. by Alaric Albertsson, also a North American) in line with the apparent trend in the Futhorc away from the more magico-religious view in the Elder Futhark. Indeed, and as I have already indicated, it could be argued (and is by the likes of Thorsson) that the development of the Younger Futhark in the Viking era (800 CE – 1100 CE) was to maintain or even re-establish these magico-religious dimensions in the advance of the more literal Roman script and alphabet, as well as dealing with any Christian 'repression'.

Of interest here is that in England there was the continued use of epigraphic stone runes in the north during the latter part of the first millennium of the CE. It is possible that the Christian Church in the north had a different view of runes and, being more distant from the Roman Church's influence, tended to be more holistic and integrative of other views and beliefs. The Church in the north was somewhat idiosyncratic, as with the views of Pelagius in the 5th century, as well as issues around tonsures and the dating of Easter raised at the Synod of Whitby in the 7th century.

Northern England, Scotland and Ireland were also the sites of Viking contact from the early 9th century, so the influence of their developments in the Younger Futhark may also have been signif-icant from at least that time, and probably before. Trade in the north between England and Scandinavia existed well before this time, which is hardly surprising for a seafaring power able to reach Greenland, Newfoundland and most probably North America many centuries before Columbus.

But, in general, there was an increasing use of the Roman script within these societies during this period, such that the Old English language becomes and is now referred to entirely in Roman script, with a couple of included anomalies, such as the retention of the **Thorn** ['th'] and **Wyn** ['p'] runes, and occasionally others, where there is some degree of overlap between the two; this would obviously have been a progressive, regional, and varied development. Although these runic inclusions have now been excluded from our modern language, they are frequently retained in Old English studies. It is of note and particular interest to me that whilst the Roman script was retained, Latin as a tongue was not: Old English has become the source of the language that dominates the globe, with its source in Indo-European via the Teutonic languages, and specifically the Anglo-Saxon tongue. Also, and equally notably, the Church succeeded politically in establishing and maintaining its influence where the Romans failed.

I contend that the more esoteric view of runes is ultimately shamanic, with this position being exemplified by Woden in a symbolic manner (see later text). In spite of the modern revival of Druidry – a somewhat aristocratic class of Celtic priesthood – that is probably over-emphasised because of ongoing and political 'awkwardness' about any Teutonic spiritual revivalism (a 'criticism' that Thorsson has experienced directly), there is a tendency toward a sanitised view of Old English spirituality as being predominantly Celtic. I consider this inaccurate and creating an unnecessary distortion. Moreover, other commentators have tried to reinstate Teutonic shamanism as a fundamental tradition in England. Brian Bates (a university academic with a PhD) has done this in *The Way of Wyrd* and, even though the work itself is fictional, it is based on good scholarly evidence.

As a slight aside, Druidry is commonly associated with the

Celts in Britain, although the Celtic migrations (also from the Germanic regions) occurred quite late (around 500 BCE). They are thus residents of the emerging Iron Age and have nothing directly to do with the Stone Age culture that produced monuments like Stonehenge. Druidry may have continuity with older priestly classes that existed prior to the Celtic migrations, but ultimately it was devastated by the Roman invasion of north-west Europe. Any survival may have been assimilated within the Anglo-Saxon culture and also become progressively Christianised.

That this shamanic influence is less obvious in England than elsewhere in northern Europe is probably partly due initially to the Roman influence, as England was the only country in our exploration that was colonised. There was also the influence of Christianity early in the Anglo-Saxon period of occupation, formally at the turn of the 7th century, though existent prior to that. Obviously Christianity did reach the northern lands, although significantly later in the millennium; this was a progressive movement, with Iceland ultimately converting democratically in 1000 CE. However, Scandinavia was a more mixed affair with conversion in some regions even later than Iceland, around the 12th century. Even with this conversion, which was often for political reasons on behalf of the indigenous authorities (and hence more token), the religious undercurrent in Teutonic cultures remained strongly pagan. It doesn't take much imagination to see the trends here with this explanation, nor that the Viking influence (including their spirituality) was more significant than has been recognised, particularly in England.

This is not to minimise the significant and dominant influence of the Christian Church, in my view, from at least a political and social perspective. Christianity has ended up the 'victor' in this domain, although the current runic revival indicates some sort of psychological redress. It is well known that the Church had a repressive stance toward religions and spiritual points of view that were not in conformity with it, such that in our current predominantly Christian society this perspective, with its inherent distortions, still holds sway. That there is a divide between the academic and esoteric positions has not been further helped by the somewhat extreme and highly speculative positions held by many in the public domain, particularly those of so-called New Age persuasion.

From a more spiritual perspective, all languages are ultimately seen to be associated with the 'word' of the gods or God. Woden (Odin in Scandinavia and Wodan in Germany) is often seen as the most significant god in the northern pantheon. Historically this has not always been so, as both Tyr and Thor had considerable influence at differing times, with Woden's significance being usually later. Woden is also the god of ecstasy and poetry (the 'word'). His self-sacrifice and discovery of the runes, as described in the Havamal (sourced in the Poetic Edda of the Viking era: see appendix) is distinctly shamanic, as well as having clear symbolic overtones comparable to the crucifixion and resurrection, which I am sure attracted the repressive tendencies of the Church. One consequence of his ordeal was the expression of eighteen charms that have mythological and runic significance. This very condensed picture of Woden can be seen to have all sorts of ramifications regarding northern spirituality generally, but also shamanism and the runes in particular.

This will be further exemplified in discussing some of the idiosyncrasies in the various rune rows. In the Elder Futhark the 4th rune is called **Ansuz** and is considered as 'a god' (commonly Odin or Wodan) on interpretation. By the time we get to the English Futhorc, the rune has become **Os** and whilst sometimes referring generically to a 'god' it is commonly inter-preted as a 'mouth', although – maybe somewhat ironically – this could be seen as Woden's poetic side. Similarly the 3rd rune **Thurisaz** can be the god Thor or a giant in the Futhark, whilst in the Futhorc it becomes **Thorn** – a 'thorn'. This trend is inter-esting; the additional runes in the Futhorc also have names that are associated with trees (oak, ash), beyond those (birch, yew) in common with the other two Futharks, as well as materials and elements (stone, fire, earth) and products (spear, bow) that are more practical and maybe for more mundane usage and communication.

The 6th rune in the Elder Futhark is **Kenaz**, which can relate to an ulcer or a sore. There are further shamanic associations here – as well as some sexual ones – with wounding, healing, and sacrifice. In the Futhorc the rune becomes **Cen** and the meaning 'a torch'. The 22nd rune **Ing** changes meaning from the northern god Ing to simply the sound 'ng' in the Futhorc. Once again, there is a demythologisation process apparent, but a further irony may be that this last rune – **Ing** – could be one source of the country named England!

Of course, that many runes refer to details such as the day, year, and sun, is no great surprise with the agricultural lifestyle and climatic conditions of the north. The seasons and their mastery, and possibly the significance of ritual and ceremonies contained in the Futharks, point to a magical and spiritual relationship to and with the land. Also the references to animals is clear, even including the now extinct aurochs (a large and wild breed of ox or bison); although it is interesting that, beyond the serpent in the expanded Futhorc, there is no reference to birds or water species of animal. There is also no reference to mythic animals or beings, nor is there any reference to supernatural beings or forces beyond the individual gods themselves. Finally, although the sun is present the moon is not.

I also find the absence of direct reference to metals interesting in an era that follows the bronze and iron ages; is this because the runes are even more ancient than we guess at? There is a reference to a spear, but not a sword. Does this reinforce the rhetorical nature of the above question, or might the last Futhorc runes of 'chalice', 'stone', and 'spear' refer to other functions? The spear is present in both the crucifixion and Odin's self-sacrifice.

The stone is both an alchemical concept and associated with king-making. The chalice, seemingly connected to Christianity and maybe a borrowed term, may also hark back to the use of the drinking horn. There are echoes here of the Arthurian corpus and the spiritual significance of the Holy Grail, which is also an alchemical motif. There are no rune poems to clarify these issues, yet they remain tantalising.

Other meanings are generally mundane and practical, at one level, though they can have a deeper and metaphoric meaning if a more esoteric perspective is taken, which is how the rune poems should be approached. From the mundane and physical levels, runic meanings can extend to the sexual, cultural, social, psychological, mythic, and spiritual domains. The possibilities seem endless, but isn't this a fundamental quality of symbolism?

Runes are presented as a pictograph, an associated letter (of the Roman alphabet), a name, sound, and a meaning; there may be several of these meanings within each rune, possibly due to levels of kenning in the rune-master and the context in which the runes are used. In general, I will not be taking a literal approach to the runes, so the alphabet associations – although academically and otherwise interesting – do not further the more symbolic perspective, so these will be minimised.

Consideration should not be lost on the pictographic aspect itself, the runes should be seen primarily as symbols in their own right. The aurochs is a wild and powerful beast; so is the shape of the Ur rune in the Futharks – Λ – that of the beast with the head down and horns protruding? For those of a more Freudian persuasion the sexual aspects may 'stick out' (pun intended). In fact, many of the runes lend themselves not only to sexual interpretation, but also to hand gestures and bodily positions for either one or two people: a western yoga and tantra perhaps?

This is the first spectrum that needs to be considered: from literal to metaphoric and then symbolic, incorporating names and meanings. But also there is a parallel perspective that I will arbitrarily define as psychological, divinatory, and magical. Psychological refers to the meaning that is commonly represented within the rune, and is the basis for the next two perspectives. The divinatory is when the runes are 'consulted' in response to a query or question; that is, when the spiritual is being asked to intercede in mundane reality (this could be loosely equated with praying). The magical approach is when the runemaster (magician or shaman) uses the runes to effect change in reality through active magical intercession in the spiritual domains.

A divinatory approach involves a 'reading', or layout of runes, in response to a query. A common method is to draw – unseen – from the rune-pouch three runes in succession. The first representing what underlies the query (the 'past'), the second where the querant or rune-master presently stands with the query (the 'present') and the third what the query is portending (the 'future'). My preference for other words than 'past' etc. indicates that the time factor here should be considered fluid and relative, and not in the linear and fixed manner we currently perceive it, otherwise we can get tangled up and confused with concepts like 'fate' and 'free will'. It is probable the Teutonic peoples also saw time in a similar and more cyclic manner.

In the divinatory method, not only should the runes be read 'psychologically' in an individual sense, but the overall pattern also be appreciated and interpreted. This orientation is expanded in one magical approach where a 'bind-rune' (usually a combination of two, three, or more runes-into-one) is used for the purposes of a charm, spell or even a curse. In this case, the runemaster selects the runes to be used and 'commits' them to a ritual process to effect change. However, there are many more varied approaches that can – obviously – be used here and would themselves have been relatively secret; which is another reason why the bequeathed runic material does not easily lend itself to a magical interpretation.

To gain a further appreciation of these areas, the writers referred to in the bibliography should be explored. Other approaches that would be useful include the fields of shamanism and the magical disciplines. I must state here, as an Englishman by birth, that one balance I am trying to redress is the accent in magical circles, from just over one hundred years ago, toward symbolic systems (such as the Tarot), languages (such as Hebrew), and magical systems (such as the Kabbalah) that may not resonate with the northern psyche. Nor might any casual indirect reference to Freud (via sexuality); Jung may be a better option, with his symbolic appreciation, mystical outlook, and theory of archetypes that approach 'the gods'. Jung was also of Germanic descent.

Taking a psychoanalytic perspective on the concept of 'repression' one step further, and beyond my comments above about the sexual interpretations: What does the modern revival have to tell us?

I suspect the modern revival is just that, a 'return of the repressed'. This would include sexuality anyway, although a more Jungian perspective would be of greater intellectual, expansive, and creative interest. The argument would go like this: We have been psychically separated from these deeper spiritual aspects of ourselves by the repressive and controlling forces within Christianity, as well as by other associated cultures. Whilst this may have suited the political and power ambitions within northern society at the time, it has and does not lead to a longer term integration, and thus our present confused position with respect to our indigenous spirituality. Even the events in 20th century Germany should be seen in this light, if properly viewed from a creative as well as the more commonly destructive and often prejudiced perspective.

Consequently there is a psychological imperative to get beyond this repression and to reconnect with these deep forces. These could be considered archetypal in Jung's terms, but to consider the pagan gods as 'just' archetypes in some sort of psychological reductionism would be a grave error – the gods are not simply archetypes. Instead we should see them as vital forces within and beyond the individual psyche, or soul, that 'demand' a hearing and to effect a reintegration; we ignore them at our peril. Should your disposition be of a fundamentally Teutonic nature, then the runes would be a valid pathway for this exploration and reunification... they could be 'for you'.

The overall understanding of runelore is of gaining a connection, a relationship, to the greater 'reality' in which we are embedded. A fundamental is that this reality is all-powerful, wise, and knowing, as in the Christian sense of 'God'. It is also eternal and infinite, such that the present contains all the spectrum of our past and future. Yet we are an expression of this greater reality in time and space, and in some mysterious way involved in its – our – evolution and consciousness.

I contend that the language of this relationship is deeply imaginative and expressed symbolically. Hence the complexity of the runes, comprising levels of image, sound, name and meaning in a multi-faceted manner that can be seen as such a language and transcending less complete systems. This complexity is fundamentally holistic ranging from the known to the mysterious, recognising that human understanding is possible, but limited.

Beyond this is an act of faith...

After these introductory remarks, I will now progress to a discussion of each individual rune of the English Futhorc.

There are several reasons for my choice: The first is my English background, but this is reinforced by the fact that for most of us Modern English is our language of choice and this connects directly with Old English that, as a script, supervened the runes. Yet even the Modern English language is occultly and subtly runic. The rune poems begin chronologically with the Old

English rune poem, if the written medium is considered; so in a way this is the 'source' material for the Futhorc that also includes the Elder Futhark, which has no corresponding poem. I have found magical exploration of the Younger Futhark to be of significant value, although I have tended in the past to use the Elder Futhark for divinatory purposes and 'work' with other people (as most commentators seem to do). However, in recent times I have gravitated to the Futhorc, which has more psychosocial significance for me, and is more expressive of my personal heritage. I am currently employed in exploring the relevance of the whole Futhark system from the perspective of being an Australian.

From a personal position, and as an Englishman now permanently resident in Australia, I see that this exploration can serve other functions. Europeans still have an uneasy relationship with this Australasian continent and particularly its spirituality. Aboriginal culture may be of value, but is probably not the avenue for ex-patriot Europeans to examine to make Australia their 'spiritual home'. Instead, I believe we need to explore our own indigenous spirituality and bring this to bear on living in Australia. In one sense, this present exploration of runelore could be seen as a beginning that could extend to deeper psychological, mythological, and cosmological perspectives, as yet unknown.

How to Use the Runes

Introduction

Personally I find 'how to' books a bit of an anomaly. I always wonder how far instruction can be given in book form, when education beyond a certain point demands more verbal, ritual, and initiatory perspectives. In this respect I am under no illusion, so I generally buy books for their intellectual and informative value, and then adapt these to my own personal development and evolutionary process. In general, I find 'how to' books to be simplistic, and sometimes both inflated and arrogant; beyond a certain point I ask myself how the author can possibly claim such authority?

Yet we are an evolving species; information exchange is both rapid and extensive. As I sit here writing I can draw upon a dictionary as well as spell-check, go online to confirm facts, and surf to follow associations and lines of thinking that arise as I write. I can draw on a font for the runes, and can also refer to books from my collection that I may have sourced and received from overseas in a matter of days. I can phone, text, email, or Skype colleagues for discussion and information. We live in a 'New Age', so I ask myself what a genuine 'how to' book may look like in this context.

Certainly I have in my background a significant educational, training, and initiatory development in the intellectual, professional, and spiritual fields. This comprises written education, but also lectures, seminars, workshops, personal therapy, spiritual instruction, rites of passage, life experience, and much more... it is in this context that I see the runes. I most certainly do not see them in the way many would use the horoscope in the paper as just some sort of simplistic guide for the day.

But firstly, why the runes? My belief is that any magical system must draw the individual to and into it. There are a range available, probably the most common being the Tarot and the I Ching. All are derived from Tradition (I use the capital here and henceforth pointedly) and therefore have the capacity to resonate within the individual at levels beyond their personal history, particularly if a more racial and collective viewpoint of inheritance is taken. During the course of my personal development I have researched and practised with all these tools, but it was the runes that drew me in.

But what does it mean to be 'drawn in'? My initial experience was that runes seemed to respond more than other methods to my divinatory questions; it was as if a dialogue with an unknown person or reality was occurring. And the more I communicated the deeper the dialogue became. This continued for quite a period, although I was very reluctant to use the runes – or anything for that matter – for operative magic. I surmised that the runes were a part of my heritage, and this has proven to be the case. I also started to 'see' things 'runically' in everyday life and runes started to appear in my dreams.

I would imagine that most of you reading this are in a similar position, although of varying levels of personal development. Beyond using the runes for personal 'amusement' (when they may not 'talk' to you anyway), I believe their exploration should be in the context of a broad personal developmental approach to life, in whatever form that takes. Mine has been most varied, eclectic, and somewhat erratic; but that suits my disposition.

Yet it is inevitable that this approach would translate into my orientation as to 'how to'. The governing disciplines in this, for me, are psychology (in its authentic sense), alchemy, shamanism, and magic (in no particular order). As a medical practitioner with a predominantly mental health orientation this suits both my personal and professional lives. From a Jungian background I see myself as a 'post-Jungian' exploring the analytic and depth psychologies in an eclectic manner. Alchemy is a discipline I believe has a wide and as yet unexplored application to mental and physical health. Shamanism, in the modern context of 'freestyle shamanism', is my drawing upon whichever disciplines and approaches that suit my disposition. Likewise with magic, where 'chaos magic' may be the term that best applies, and for which the runes are my primary tool in the operative sense.

Yes, I have stepped into and now practise operative magic, and this 'how to' will guide you to this position. However, beyond a certain point you are on your own, hence some of my earlier comments about personal experience and development. In this respect I can only provide an educative background and guidance to this point for each reader individually, which will be governed by your personal development and maturity – beyond that you are on your own.

And this is how I have tried to write *Just Add Blood* to date. I have left a lot out, partly because there is a lot missing and maybe never to be retrieved, also partly because some of the dots I have joined up are instruction, leaving gaps for you to join others. But mainly because that is the nature of the beast: it is a vast jigsaw with some constellations, a lot of gaps, as well as having a border that has not yet been clearly defined – or should possibly never be.

I will try to be progressive from this educative position I have outlined to date. Initially the approach from here will be instructive and relatively simple, but as we progress the process will overtake any structure and become more fluid. At some point, and progressively thereafter, your own experience will come increasingly to the fore. Any ideas and intuitions you may have are totally valid, as working with a system that is greater than your own will guide you increasingly. So you may get to a point in this 'how to' section where you need my guidance no longer, and that is totally valid.

So, let's step into this vast sea...

Getting to Know the Runes

Have you got a rune set? If you have, it is most likely to be one of the Elder Futhark; check by counting and comparing the images as with the **Cen/Kenaz/Kaun** 6th rune, most particularly. If you haven't, and because I am working with the extended Futhorc, then try to obtain the 33-rune version. It may be a little early to make your own, but if not here, ultimately it is the thing to do; particularly if you find the runes 'talk' to you, and certainly if you are going to use them for operative magic. You may end up with more than one set and possibly use them for different purposes. But, in the meantime, there is the creative possibility of drawing and sketching the runes, and so familiarising yourself with them in this manner.

Carry them with you, play with them, take them into different settings... and, as you do this, explore your feelings and responses. Draw one, try to see what it means to you and if it 'talks' in any way. Then refer to this book, or any other that you may have or may be appropriate for you, and/or for the purpose of the consultation.

There are at least two ways you can make progress in this process. One is contemplate a rune each day in sequential order, starting with **Feoh**, then carry it with you and explore its meanings both intuitively and educatively. The other would be to draw a random rune for each day and undertake the same examination, then see how the rune and meaning 'applies' to that day.

From this point you might want to follow your nose with further exploration, such as on the internet (be careful, there is a lot of rubbish out there!), or to other disciplines that may contain information for you to be able to expand your appreciation. For example, as I was writing the preceding section, a series of programmes on the Viking Age came on the television, so I was able to cross-reference my writing with another viewpoint, as well as gaining some additional information. This was a synchronicity, which I would see as both relevant and part of the communication process.

Wherever your nose leads you...

Divination

From this point on you will definitely need a rune set and a pouch to contain them. I'm also going to keep this section fairly simple with only two methods, and leave it to you to explore other permutations and combinations. One reason for this is that I want to emphasise the ground that should be covered to this point of exploration, so you do not enter into the divinatory process in a trivial manner.

At the very least, I would have expected you to explore the meanings outlined. I am fully aware there are much simpler outlines available; but the study and discipline, plus your own exploration, will stand you in good stead. If the runes haven't 'talked' to you by now, then maybe they are not for you, and any divination process is likely to be unhelpful and – particularly if the god Loki is involved – be inaccurate, misleading, or downright mischievous in where you may be led. Be warned.

First method
The first method is an extension of the above familiarisation process and permits the drawing of a single rune in response to a question.

The question is important and, again, should not be trivial – unless you want a trivial reply. A good question is often one that has palpable emotional significance to and for you, and you may even be anxious about the answer, although these are all good signs. In general this should be a question for which you don't have a clear response in your mind already. You may want to write it out. But, at the very least I suggest you take yourself and your runes to a setting that is significant (we will talk more about this when we come to rituals), and then speak the question out aloud. Then close your eyes and draw a single rune from the pouch by feeling around and taking the rune you are 'drawn' to in a psychic way; this rune may make itself known or be otherwise 'obvious' to you.

Then examine the rune with whatever knowledge and experience you have to date, and see how much it addresses your question and how you are affected by it. You may want to leave the space and explore the rune further in a journal (again, we'll come to this), with information from these pages and any other sources relevant to you.

Second method

The second method is one I prefer, and has historical reference. It is also the one I use if ever I am doing a 'reading' for someone. A reading is simply that I perform the function of drawing and interpreting the runes in response to the question posed by the questioner. It is not always essential that I know what the question is to do this; in fact, and sometimes obviously, it can be a hindrance to do so.

In this case the initial stages are the same, except three runes are drawn and laid out left to right, sight unseen. The first rune represents, in literal terms, the past. In metaphoric terms, and hence of deeper significance, it is the ground, legacy, or heritage of a personal and historical nature on which you stand with respect to the question. The second is the present, or where you stand right now with respect to the question. The third is the future, or where the question and the runic responses to date are leading you; the image here is the horizon.

Past, present and future put the sequence in a linear time framework, which I find somewhat limited. The second appreciation, with its images of what you stand upon, where you are standing right now, and what you are looking out onto, are more significant to my mind. They bring all these facets of linear time into the present rather than seeing the outcome fatalistically, offering some sort of response and interaction in the ritual process; this itself is an act of magic.

The process from here is then as the first method, above.

From this point adopt a 'freestyle' shamanic attitude and explore other methods of divination. Many commentators will give you alternatives, and you may draw from other disciplines; for example, Tarot readings have reading methods that can be applied.

However, be careful about over-complicating the process. Intuitively I am drawn to mandala-like readings, as I have a sense this is the sort of patterning that the magical reality 'understands' and can express itself to us through. I also enjoy simplicity, so it is rare that I stray from the methods I have outlined here.

The Rune Journal

Initially, I am going to assume that you are not familiar with a diary or journal process, although I appreciate many or most readers would be. However, I will start with this assumption and lead into other possibilities from there.

In the broader context the use of a journal has become almost indispensable for the personal growth process, and as the runes are used for this purpose, the orientation I will take for any 'beginner' in this area will be in this wider context. If you have arrived at this point and do not use a journal, I would advise that you start one to record your experiences and outcomes with the divinatory process, at least.

The journal itself could be quite simple, like a notebook. Although giving the process a little more sanctity could be facilitated by using one of those blank bound diaries that are now readily available at gift shops and newsagents. Clearly date and record your experiences, and make note of the surrounding circumstances. What drew you to asking this question? What does the reading tell you, and how do you intend to apply it?

These questions inevitably lead into a wider process; the above reflections demand a context of your life, thoughts and feelings, directions and plans. This is set in a web of associations, such as partnership, family, work and friends, and the wider psychosocial context these are embedded in. In this context a journal is a reflective tool, a place where you can express your most personal thoughts, feelings, and their consequences. I would add dreams with reflections about them, as well as any unusual experiences or happenings, such as synchronistic occurrences.

Reflections on personal history are welcome, but more pertinent if initiated by circumstances and events, and always in the context of the 'present'. Creative additions, poetic utterances, and quotes from other sources are all potentially valuable additions. This is a place where you can be most intimate with yourself, so please keep the journal safe from prying eyes; you may even protect it with a rune such as **Eolh**, or an appropriate bind-rune.

Many of you would already have a journal process happening, most probably with additions I have not mentioned here, but if you have not then following the above steps will let you catch up with those who do, and provide a platform to further develop your own journal and the journal process. For example, as I usually get up to write early, I have a computer file which I can use as a broad journal, particularly because at this hour any dreams are more immediate and the time of day facilitates reflectiveness. I have a range of other notebooks and pads that I use as an extension of this; some are for specified purposes, particularly rune and magical work, but also notes of ideas, poetry, drawings and paintings, and the like.

The good alchemist always makes a record of his experiments and their outcomes. This is equivalent and your journal contains – is – your own alchemical process, into which magical operations will be included and even direct the process.

Ritual

The journal process is a ritual; rituals were not discarded in the nursery. At times of stress and strain they emerge in often primitive and child-like form, indicating their potential place in dealing with turbulence and transition. Other cultures preserve rituals in an extant form that often appeal emotionally when we visit them; we then experience their absence in our busy, preoccupied lives. We ignore them at our emotional peril.

Reading the runes is a ritual. As with all rituals the process itself should be in a conducive setting, maybe one sourced and set apart for this purpose, or a routine space sanctified by an act of dedication. The setting is important, as is your place in it. You may find it necessary to bathe (a ritual of purification) and dress for the occasion, even using specific clothing, such as robes, and any amulets. If others join you in any ritual process then it becomes more ceremonial, particularly if one of the assembled number conducts a ritual with the others participating.

A ritual setting is sacred. The setting may have objects of reverence placed there prior to the ritual, such as swords and chalices. The elements may be represented by salt (earth), water in a vessel, a feather (air) and burning incense placed in the appropriate quarters of a designated circle. A task for you is to work out which element and/or icon goes with which quarter. The circle may then be sanctified by casting it with a wand or staff, walking or circling sun-wise from the east and back to the east again. Each quarter may then be blessed and dedicated. Then the ritual process may occur. Afterward the process is reversed with the circle unwound, and the sacred space metaphorically dispersed.

This may all sound overwhelming if you are not familiar with rituals. However, I hope the above gives you enough information to start and experiment. Please do not neglect the imaginative process, which can augment and elaborate on the ritual structure, as well as being used at alternative times when appropriate.

Imagination, in general, has a wide application in this whole domain and is the basis of any 'freestyle' shamanism.

Of course, there is much more that could be said about ritual, as well as further instruction. This is properly a separate piece of writing, but I believe the above is sufficient for starters, and I can't stress enough your own participation and experimentation. With the wonders of modern technology, you may easily search and research more, but an earlier caveat applies: be very discerning, there is a lot of poor quality material and instruction on the internet, and some may be downright misleading, if not potentially malicious. It will serve you well to develop your 'magical muscles' from your own inner resources first – plus a little help from the runes and the gods.

Magic

By now you will have recognised that there is no 'pure stream' of runic magic. The runes themselves, as seen in the introduction, are set in a wide context of history, culture, religion, mythology, and cosmology, as well as their social and psychological reflections. The magic of the runes emerges from the broad complex known as shamanism and is a significant component in the various streams of magic that we now know of in the modern era. Some of these, such as the Kabbalah, have many different cultural and religious roots, making their compatibility difficult, if not confusing and even impossible. However, in the modern era there is a cross-fertilisation process amongst all these Traditions, with the impetus to globalisation and the similarity of archetypal roots.

To this heady mix I personally add alchemy, as it was a Tradition of the ages of metal and their use; although we now tend to see it in mediaeval form, as a process it is of great assistance to both magic and shamanism. Also psychology is a modern art that should not be forgotten. I am eschewing the academic and clinical branches here and focussing more on the depth traditions (Jung, Reich etc.), because I believe these depth psychologies provide a valuable link to the other Traditions and magic. Indeed, as magic is going feral with concepts such as 'chaos magic' and shamanism with 'freestyle shamanism', I believe alchemy could gain some flexibility and freedom, particularly in the healing arts. And I think that the depth psychologies are in a transitional state where a healthy injection of these other disciplines may provide much in the way of cross-fertilisation.

Indeed, I see that depth psychology is a fundamental in what I would call 'lesser magic'. In its application to personal growth and development, depth psychology provides the tools of inner reflection that can help consolidate the individual 'self', or soul, distinct from life's vicissitudes. Of course, there is a healthy mix of alchemy and shamanism in this (particularly if a therapeutic process is undertaken), but this art can in itself be a ritual of initiation and a rite of passage.

Lesser magic has a parallel in divination, in contrast to operative or 'greater magic'. It is more receptive and reflective, even 'feminine', like the soul itself. But it is an essential precursor to its greater cousin. Without it the individual is susceptible to calamities, such as the 'soul loss' and 'spirit possession' of shamanism, that are all too apparent in modern mental hospitals under the haze of drugs and medical control. There is – obviously – much more that could be said here, but the message is obvious: Do your personal development work otherwise magic will undo you.

Rune Magic

The fundamental principle here requires an act of faith: that the 'reality' being communicated with and participated in by the magician is greater and more intelligent than the individual. And that magic is the process of forming an active relationship with this reality, of which we are an expression, for the purpose of being involved in the creative and evolutionary process. This bears a great responsibility and is laden with obvious pitfalls; yet the demand has been there throughout human evolution, and I would contend that is a responsibility not to be shirked.

Psychology, as illustrated above, is the receptive arm of the process and divination part of its expression. There is a passivity in this 'lesser magic' that is transcended as we move into the greater and operative realms to participate co-creatively in the evolutionary journey. At one level this 'reality' always remains mysterious and transcends even the evolution in which we are involved, yet seems to demand our involvement in the process. I will stop at this point; we are at the borders of mysticism here, and our interest is primarily in the magical process and the use of the runes in particular.

In these respects the runes are not seen as man's invention, but as a gift of the gods. This paradoxical relationship is amplified in Woden's self-sacrifice where, pierced by a spear, he hung for nine days and nights on a tree. In this ritual ordeal he retrieved the runes and expressed them in eighteen charms. This poetic myth is worth exploring in some detail as it contains much that we have been talking about. However, it is not an instruction manual for the operative use of the runes, but riddles about their meaning. It was the responsibility of rune-masters to 'translate' this material into an understanding of the runes and apply this magically.

This is one reason why the background appreciation of the runes and the process of divination are both important prelimi-naries, but also important as an ongoing background to any operative work. I feel my appreciation of the runes is in a constant state of evolution, and that this appreciation will change and mature, even as I write this work. In this sense we are all Woden and constantly undergoing the sacrificial process.

The essential change in operative magic is that the rune-master chooses the runes and how to use them. The issues and questions may be the same; that is, they are being used in response to some inner demand or external circumstance, including, in the shamanic sense, for another or others. The ones used may even be selected from a divinatory type of process ('drawing'), rather than self-selection from your knowledge of each.

As with divination this may be single or multiple. For example, a rune may be carved into a wooden stave or etched in a stone to be worked with in ritual and maybe carried as a talisman, amulet, or otherwise sacrificed to earth, wind, water, or fire. More runes may be used for a more comprehensive 'picture' and here some may be 'bound' into a combined runic form called a bind-rune. Bind-runes are often used as charms or for spells – even curses. As you can intuit here, our motives in such acts must be well examined and responsibility for any outcome recognised.

I am going to draw a line in the sand here; it must be done somewhere after all. Because, and as explained, this work is difficult to convey in this written means of communication beyond a certain point. And for many, this point may have been reached a while ago, yet for others the desire for more is still present.

Some issues have not been discussed; for example, the making of runes (although some initial reflection on this will follow). Others, such as bind-runes, above, could be extended considerably. The academic and scholarly input has provided authenticity and a necessary depth to the field, but could be taken further. So I am left with the question of where to take it all?

There will be a further works, exploring specifically rune magic, in the context of magic generally and the related fields of shamanism, depth psychology, and alchemy. From a practical perspective, any progress in this and related fields I will express on my website.

The most obvious development from here, and the loose strands I have left, is more Traditional. It would involve rune-making with accompanying guidelines drawn from the above. It could extend to instruction and participation in a variety of formats.

For these any associated developments, I suggest you look up my website.

2

The Anglo-Saxon Futhorc

Introduction

Earlier I made the comment that 'from the mundane and physical levels, runic meanings can extend to the sexual, cultural, social, psychological, mythic, and spiritual'. But even this could represent an incomplete list; for example, emotions, the body, as well as both physical and mental health, could be easily added. It seems to me that most descriptions of runes that offer some sort of interpretation are a smorgasbord of meanings picked from some or all of these levels. The more the interpretations approach the 'daily horoscope' mentality, the more they lose the depth and magic that is the essence of the runes.

I am basing this exploration on the English Futhorc and will use the Bruce Dickins translation of the Old English rune poem from the transcript that George Hickes made of the original in 1705. This original was lost in a fire in 1731, so it is not known for certain whether the assignment of the poetic riddles to individual runes is entirely authentic. However, there is good agreement with the Scandinavian rune poems for the 16 common runes, and it is generally considered in academic circles that the correspondences are valid.

It should not be forgotten that the rune poem is considered to derive from a prior oral existence, originating from some time in the 8th and 9th centuries, committed to writing by a Christian scribe in the 10th century, and preserved in the manuscript destroyed by the fire of 1731. The pagan influences in the recorded script were undoubtedly significant, and some attempt would have been made to either 'exorcise' or otherwise modify them following the Christianisation that proceeded in England from the early 7th century. However, from the spiritual perspective there is less conflict between the two religious orientations, which is also my feeling about the Christian influence in the poem, so there would need to be some discernment here with interpretation. Also the rune poem describes only 29 runes, and it has already been indicated that the last four runes have some spiritual connotations that may be common to both Christianity and the pagan traditions it superseded.

Each riddle will accompany the assigned rune. I will try to use a standard graphic representation of each rune, although there are variations noted by Hickes in some of them. These variations could be considered to occur depending on their source, as well as changes over time. I will mention the Scandinavian rune poems where they offer a significant contrast that will inform us further (which is relatively frequently).

If this overall assessment were considered from a historical perspective in terms of authenticity, then there would be room for argument about issues such as accuracy and validity. However, this – my – perspective should be seen as relative, as the information we have to hand is only a very small portion of what would have been produced. In other words, and being imaginative, there would have been other variations on the shapes of runes; different assignments; other poems and riddles, as well as much that is mundane, uneducated, and could be considered as graffiti – unworthy of the academic attention it might otherwise receive.

More important to our study is the magical dimension. In reconnecting to the runic corpus, I am following a fluid and creative tradition in the company of other similar travellers. The assignments and their interpretations could be considered part of this magical process of reconnection with a spiritual tradition in a modern age, which will inevitably change and develop over time.

My emphasis from this point will be primarily psychological in the authentic sense of 'soul'. I will focus on the physical, sexual, emotional, and intellectual aspects from the poem, and draw upon various interpretations of runes I have read elsewhere. However, the resulting synthesis and many of the insights will be my own with all the attendant subjectivity. The social and cultural aspects in the poem are obviously historical, so some modernisation will need to be employed on occasion.

The mythological levels are significant, but are more prevalent and unsullied in the continental material of the Elder Futhark. The relevance of English 'mythology' (whatever that may be and a subject in its own right) in the Futhorc is less by comparison because of other influences, such as the indigenous culture that greeted the Anglo-Saxon immigrants, and the comparatively early influence of the Roman Church; although it remains of interest from at least a symbolic perspective. Where this comparison causes a differing rendering in the content of the poems, such as with a name (as has already been discussed with Woden), I will offer the appropriate alternatives according to whichever rune poem is being referred to at the time.

Collectively, this psychological approach satisfies the more 'meaning' and divinatory aspects of rune usage that, as stated, I am undertaking from an individual or 'soul' perspective. However, there is also a spiritual perspective embedded in all of the material, which is more apparent when the runes are employed for magical purposes. Here I suffer some of the difficulties and restrictions that would have affected early commentators, in that such an approach and the material employed is more ritualistic and conveyed best in oral tradition and its initiatory transmission. In this spiritual respect the occult meaning of the runes as 'mysteries' comes to the fore.

The principle authors I have used as a background to these interpretations are Edred Thorsson, Freya Aswynn, and Jan Fries. This is a kind of cherry-picking of intellectual, intuitive, and imaginative perspectives, although the resultant synthesis is more distinctly based on my poetic appreciation of the rune poems, plus a bit of creativity (a gift from the gods). I believe this is in the spirit of the runes in our time and meets a demand both personal and cultural.

Runes of the Elder Futhark rune row are set out in 'aetts', or three groups each containing eight runes. The Futhorc follows this, although the definition is less pronounced after the 24th rune. Each aett is considered to be headed and named by the first rune of the series, and to have some common characteristics. These features will be described at the conclusion of each aett.

The authentic pictographic representation (inasmuch as this is possible) of each rune of the Futhorc will head each description. If the Elder Futhark version varies significantly, I will provide the alternative in a slightly smaller form next to the original. This is because you may have, or may only be able to obtain, the Elder Futhark version.

There will be no description of reversed or inverted runes; this is a modern derivation, or deviation, as is the so-called 'blank' rune (of the so-called 'self' rune) that provides a subtle Christianisation already apparent enough. There are various ways of using the runes that take more than sufficient account of features like reversal, resulting in a greater and more comprehensive range of meaning, that render such descriptions irrelevant and even counter-productive.

There is enough to do to fill in the gaps that exist with the scant amount of information at our modern disposal without complicating and obfuscating the overall picture with personal psychological projections. My belief is that we start with what is extant and given, gain the wisdom of modern commentators who have explored runes from this basis, and then add a healthy dose of intuition and speculation – including your own.

To my mind this represents an authentic basis from which to explore the runes, modernise them, and give them a trajectory into the future. I believe this represents an active – magical – relationship with the runes and the greater forces that stand behind them, rather than imposing our own psychology on them and the – very modern – desire to make order beyond what exists.

A final point before discussing the runes further: I am not going to describe them in neat categories directed toward meaning, be they divinatory or magical (or even – woe to you – academic). I have approached each rune in a contemplative state and written 'around' them from my prior knowledge and understanding.

I have only paid limited attention to the phonetic and etymological aspects of the runes. Although of academic and intellectual interest, I find such approaches take me too far away from the essence and symbolic expression of the runes into modernity, and they also represent a continuation of the sort of influences I am trying to both differentiate and relatively excise from the core 'meanings'.

From the reader's – your – perspective, I would suggest that you will gain most value from my rendering by approaching each rune in this contemplative manner: read 'around' what I have expressed; skip to any reference to other material (such as the other rune poems) that may be mentioned and captures your interest, and then try to get a mature 'feeling', derived from any thoughts and emotions, of what the rune – or series of runes – means to you in the context of any question you may have posed.

So to the runes and the first aett of Feoh:

42

Runes Common to the Elder Futhark

Runes I – 24

ᚠ

Feoh

Wealth, Cattle

Wealth is a comfort to all men;
yet must everyman bestow it freely,
if he wish to gain honour in the sight of the lord.

'Lord' here may be seen in a Christian manner rather than referring to a physical person, yet paradoxically it accords with pagan tradition and a physical lord as well. Although a little harsher, using the word 'discord', the Scandinavian poems carry a similar sentiment. However, the Icelandic rune poem also refers to wealth as 'fire of the sea' and 'path of the serpent'. The actual runic image could be of a person with arms stretched outward and upward in an act of religious supplication and receptivity.

Cattle is historic in meaning, the original indicator and maybe arbiter of wealth in pagan times. Wealth can be seen here as energy and the need for its circulation, otherwise it brings trouble – discord. In the internal sense this is personal value, a person's rank or standing, and maybe another kenning of 'honour in the sight of the lord'.

Other associations are fire and gold. Fire of the sea would indicate strong emotion, even sexual energy, reinforced by the 'path of the serpent' in the Icelandic poem, which recalls the kundalini energy of eastern mysticism. Mythologically gold directs us toward Freyja, or Freo in English, who is a goddess of the water, and hence 'fire of the sea'. 'Tears of the sea' is a complementary phrase that refers to amber, also valuable and attributable to Freyja/Freo. A goddess of the Vanir family or race, who were often at war with the Aesir (or the race of gods, headed by Woden), she also – paradoxically – taught Odin/Woden seidr/seith or magic of the 'seething' kind, being the visionary and even sexual variety of the art. The Brisingamen necklace that Freyja/Freo adorned was obtained from the four dwarves who made it and subsequently gave it to her in return for sexual favours – with each of them on successive nights – when she coveted it.

Feoh is rich, powerful, and the goddess of fertility – and sexuality. But the warning is to be generous with wealth and to involve others in any largess. **Feoh** concerns the cultivation of feminine energies and skills, with a strong association to fertility, magic, and witchcraft.

Ո

Ur
Aurochs

The aurochs is proud and has great horns:
it is a savage beast and fights with its horns;
a great ranger of the moors, it is a creature of mettle.

The aurochs, a primitive ox or bison, is now extinct, dying out early in the second millennium. It represents a wild, primal force, as it was unable to be tamed. Indeed it was a challenge to young men to slay one, and the garnered horns represent the resultant trophy. The rune can then be seen as a ritual or rite of passage for men in a culture where courage and strength were highly valued. The horns, represented in the image, would be used for drinking (both socially and ritually). The runic image could also be seen as phallic, whichever way it is viewed.

The word 'ur' as a prefix means original or primitive and

refers to the core primal energy of a predominantly masculine variety. There is thus a subtle pairing of the first two runes at this energetic masculine-feminine level. Scratch the surface of meanings and the sexual connotations are both distinct and intense.

By contrast, in the Scandinavian rune poems the **Ur** rune refers to rain, drizzle, and even slag. Although often seen in a cleansing light, this meaning points to the harsh conditions of the north, as well as referring to the primal mythic and cosmological levels of the Scandinavian peoples: ice is a major component of their creation myths. A tangential view is that all these associations point to **Ur** being semen, which supports the phallic and sexual interpretation.

Ur is raw primal energy and vitality; it is the wild side of our nature that is untamed yet also the basis of our consciousness through our instinctual nature, here seen in a powerful yet creative light.

The subtle gender pairing extends to the primal dyad of fire and ice, the combined energies of which were the source of creation in Germanic mythology. This often dualistic pairing weaves its way down the first series or aett of the Futhorc, as will be seen with the runes that follow, and remains suggestive throughout.

The phrase 'sight of the lord' would be an interesting one if the implied 'he' is a 'she' instead. In the modern revivalism of witchcraft, called Wicca, the primal pairing is the lord and lady. The lord in Wicca is a horned god, as is the aurochs, indicating another association to this primal pairing. In mythic lore Freo's partner (or brother) is Frey, a Vanic god. It may be stretching the association to see Frey associated with the **Ur** rune, but it makes for interesting speculation.

þ

Thorn

Giant, Thorn

The thorn is exceedingly sharp,
an evil for any knight to touch,
uncommonly severe on all who sit among them.

In Germanic cosmology the giants preceded the gods and man, yet remain as part of the world. The giants represent the forces of chaos and it is Thor ('thunder') who keeps them under control. In psychological terms the giants represent the 'subconscious', those forces at the borderline of awareness that we need to keep in check. It is interesting that it is Thor who does this because, although he is a god, he has many of the giants' features. This controlling power is represented by the hammer of Thor, often worn as an amulet against the dominance of these primal forces, so contrasting the use of the Christian cross used in protection from evil; or, more pertinently, the symbolic force used to deal with it.

The Scandinavian rune poems recognise the giants to be a danger to women, presumably because of their voracious sexual appetites. In this connection, the giant is not unlike an incubus, considered evil by the Church. Maybe it is this demonic side of the rune that threatens the establishment order and why, apart from the reference to 'evil thing', the rune is edited severely and transforms to a plant in the Futhorc. I would further question whether the 'evil thing for any knight to touch' could also have later Christian misogynistic overtones.

Although harsh and somewhat severe, the Old English rune poem carries less of the severity of the other poems or their inherent meaning within the Scandinavian Futharks. There is a progressive demythologisation of the runes from this point onwards and **Thorn** marks the tone of this trend. This can be seen within the image, where the primal association with thunder becomes the thorn of a plant, readily seen in the shape of the rune.

It may be that the magical overtones here are that thorns can be a hedge that marks a boundary between civilisation and the wild, so providing a symbolic similarity between the differing runic systems. But it is one that can be crossed over, hence the fear of giants amongst women, and the implication in other texts that the magician is often a 'fence-sitter' (in Druidry he or she is known as a 'hedge-druid'). The magician is thus capable of travelling into territory that others would not dare to enter.

Thorn is therefore at the borderline of human consciousness and represents the fears of the instinctual and primal emotional forces that stand in the realms beyond yet also within the human. Significantly Thor, one who appears almost of their own kind, maintains this balance. Despite all of this, **Thorn** is considered a dangerous rune and is often utilised in spells and curses.

Os
God, Mouth

The mouth is the source of all language,
a pillar of wisdom and a comfort to wise men,
a blessing and joy to every knight.

As a brief aside, the misogynistic trend continues and further indicates the influence of Christianity within the rune poem. By contrast the Icelandic poem exemplifies Odin/Woden in his threefold – magical – form.

In fact it is difficult to read this stanza of the rune poem without its Christian influence. The Icelandic poem talks of the

God as Allfather (a common title for Odin/Woden), prince of Asgard (the dwelling of the Aesir gods), and lord of Valhalla (where warriors killed in battle go to, a kind of 'heaven'). Maybe it was this association that conflicted with the Christian perspective. However, by way of a contrast the Norse poem refers to an estuary, the 'mouth' of a river and a scabbard; being the repository of the sword that is often synonymous with the soul of the warrior (see the rune **Rad** that follows).

Yet the runic influence of Odin/Woden remains, as earlier referred to, in his capacity as the god of poetry and galdor (rune and poetic magic, the province of Odin/Woden and the complement of seidr/seith, the witchcraft of the Vanir goddess Freyja/Freo). Both poetry and rune magic employ language – words – and I have earlier referred to the association of the word with the divine. The image itself in the Old English poem reinforces the mouth, when the horizontal strokes are seen as lips in the act of speaking.

Yet all these rather 'mixed messages' are overcome when we see this rune to relate to consciousness ('pillar of wisdom') and to have moved beyond the borderline image of the **Thorn** rune. In this respect the **Os** rune represents the end of the evolution of the primal forces through the giants into the gods... next we will come to man. In this capacity **Os** represents the divine within us – the transcendent self.

Both the **Thorn** and **Os** runes overtly display a more transpersonal, mythic and cosmological quality that is not as evident in **Feoh** and **Ur**. It is as if they 'stand behind and beyond' our human existence and the primal forces of creation, yet reinforce and influence it significantly.

R

Rad

Riding

Riding seems easy to every warrior while he is indoors
and very courageous to him who traverses the high-roads
on the back of a stout horse

At the mundane level the meaning of **Rad** seems obvious: it encapsulates riding, the rider, the riding vehicle (horse) and the road. The image itself portrays a movement to the right, appearing like a figure walking.

The significance of the horse is important; it even occupies a special place as the 19th rune, Eh (horse), which is paired with the 20th rune Mann (man) in the Futhorc. The relationship between a man (a warrior in the poem) and his horse is important, although in the poem the horse is – needs to be – stout. The Scandinavian rune poems reinforce the stress involved, with riding being 'the worst thing for horses' and 'toil of the steed' in the Norse and Icelandic poems respectively.

Yet there is more implied here: the journey is not just physical, it is also spiritual. Woden rides a great eight-legged steed across the sky, reinforcing this connection. The difference is that Woden journeys between the worlds, rather than a linear journey in just physical reality. This might explain the reference to the 'finest sword' in the Norse poem, which is an extension of the comments above in **Os**. For the warrior the sword is synonymous with, or the repository of, his soul, and the journey would therefore be between the worlds and ultimately to Valhalla at the completion of his time on earth... preferably killed in battle.

After the more transpersonal images and meanings of the preceding two runes, and their derivation from primal opposites that create both them (gods and giants, among other beings) and we humans, the runes have arrived – **Rad** – at a more personal theme with the image of a journey. Such a journey requires a 'stout horse' that may be, literally, the body in physical reality. But beyond this, the horse may also be – like Woden's – the vehicle that contains all our consciousness rests upon, being the soul.

In this respect the **Rad** rune is fundamentally shamanistic. And with the association to Woden points to the galdor aspect of magic, although extending to seith magic, which will be more apparent as we move to the **Cen** rune.

K $\langle$

Cen
Torch, Light

The torch is known to every man by its pale, bright flame;
it always burns where princes sit within.

Rather like the **Ur** rune, when compared to the other rune poems **Cen** appears to demonstrate two clear meanings; here that is of a torch, yet in the other poems it is an ulcer or sore. However, this divergence diminishes significantly when the more metaphorical, symbolic and sacred levels of interpretation are explored.

The connecting point between the two meanings is the focus on death with 'death makes a corpse pale' (Norse), and 'abode of mortification' (Icelandic), both following the common phrase 'fatal to children'. The reference to death in the Old English rune poem is hinted at by 'pale, bright flame'. At the obvious level, death in childhood would have been a feature of the times, although the same poem extends this to burning and where 'princes sit within'. Again, at the obvious level this may refer to the torch and burning as cremation, but does it refer to more, as with the 'burning' of a sore or ulcer? Is 'prince' symbolic of inner richness and 'within' a reference to inner, spiritual development? It is here that we step into the shamanic level of kenning, a word that is based on **Cen**. In this framework wounding, disease and death are seen as steps of transformation facilitated by the 'inner fire'; which reminds us of kundalini or sexual energy, and the catalytic process of change in alchemy. It is my understanding that this is the core complex of meaning that **Cen** represents.

Added to this perception is that there may also be a sexual component, and that the images may refer to the core of sexuality within the woman: the kundalini reference above reinforces this. There are also three manifestations of this rune as an image: the one above as **Cen**; the Younger Futhark **Kaun** rendered with the angular stave moving upward and outwards to the right as a mirror of **Cen** around the horizontal plane, and the Elder Futhark **Kenaz** where these two angular staves join as a 'C' without the vertical stave (as seen above).

More than most of the runes, **Cen** indicates the complexity in and wisdom of the Futharks. Although beyond our capacity here, this rune has sufficient inherent information for a wide and deep level of exploration that could then reveal a methodology and wisdom for all the runes, even if it involves some filling in of gaps with intuitive guesswork.

Rad and **Cen** form a complementary and shamanic pair. As with all these pairings of the first aett it is of value to read them together to gain some of the subtleties of meaning that each contains within the other, rather like the Taoist Yin and Yang.

Gyfu

Gift

Generosity brings credit and honour, which support one's dignity;
it furnishes help and subsistence
to all broken men who are devoid of all else.

There are no correspondences to this rune poem in the Scandinavian rune poems; it is one of the eight runes that are dropped from the Elder Futhark in the composition of the later Younger version. Some of the wisdom of this reduction can be seen in the poem itself, where there are some inherent similarities to **Feoh** and more particularly **Cen**. This indicates that in this process of reduction the meaning of **Gyfu**, and hence other deleted runes, are incorporated within the remaining runes.

From the word associations in the various Germanic tongues, this rune is seen as representing a gift. In the social sense, and reinforced in **Feoh**, this can be seen as the gift of generosity and its reciprocation. At a somewhat deeper level of meaning it can relate to the giving and taking of relationship, and hence its common symbolic application to love and marriage, as indicated in the rune image itself. **Gyfu** is therefore commonly used in a bind-rune complex.

The 'broken man' brings us back to shamanism. In **Gyfu** the gift of generosity is that of the gods, or spiritual world, to mankind. It can then be seen as a rune of wounding and healing, and reinforces the shamanic theme that runs through all the Futharks. The wounding of the broken man can be physical, but even in modern parlance it may imply the breakdown in the mental realms. This is one of the profound tenets of shamanism, painting a different picture of where the modern notion of a 'mental breakdown' may lead, and how it can be dealt with in a healing manner by the 'generosity' of the gods; that is, that the spiritual world is the one that ultimately heals mental distress.

The converse notion of gift is of sacrifice. Here there is a subtle appreciation that any gift of healing – from the gods – implies a sacrifice on 'their' part. Hence the reason for the co-operative relationship with the spiritual world and the sacrifice we give – maybe only in token or symbolic form – in ritual and ceremony. Indeed, Odin/Woden's sacrifice of himself led to the discovery of the runes for mankind. The self-sacrifice of Jesus should not be forgotten in this light.

Þ

Wyn
Joy, Pleasure

Bliss he enjoys who knows not suffering, sorrow nor anxiety, and has prosperity and happiness and a good enough house.

Wyn also has no Scandinavian rune poem correspondence and seems relatively obscure. The rune shape seems an upward progression of **Thorn** and has a somewhat humanised appearance if looked at in differing ways. The word itself also lends itself to a sexual interpretation with the literal interpretation of 'winning' and 'winsome'.

This sexual aspect underlies the idea of ecstasy and leads to the shamanic dimension, almost by definition, as the shaman is considered the master of the art of ecstasy. In this respect the god who may be associated with **Wyn** is Woden, and even the runic name has a certain similarity. Of further interest is that **Wyn** has the same root as the Latin 'Venus' (goddess of love) and the race of the Vanir, of whom the goddess Freo, with all her sexual and pleasurable connections, is a member. You may recall that it was Freo who taught Woden seith, or magic that includes the sexual

– tantric – variety. All these connections are tantalising, as well as providing a distinctly different flavour to much that has been encountered so far in the rune poems.

The shamanic element is reinforced by the first line of the poem, where bliss or ecstasy could be seen as the transformation of 'suffering', 'sorrow' and 'anxiety', rather than their exclusion: Suffering is the more mental aspect of pain, as sorrow is of grief, and anxiety is in a direct manner. So we are dealing here with the more mental and spiritual aspects of existence, although a 'good enough house' could refer to the body. I suspect it implies a balance of wealth and prosperity, as implied elsewhere in the runes.

Wyn may also refer to the aspect of Woden that is most magical; that is, the exercise of the 'will'. In magical and shamanic terms the employment of the will is seen as essential. In our modern era, with its 'metapsychology', the will is often equated with the 'ego' and the latter given a somewhat deprecatory view. This is unfortunate, and where psychology can be a tool of an establishment that would disempower the individual, as the correct use of the will is essential to personal growth and transformation, which is the very essence of magic.

Gyfu and **Wyn** form a pair and have similarities, rather than some of the contrasts of the earlier pairings. They also provide a lightness and an optimism that is often lacking in the preceding runes, as well as having a more distinct sexual, magical, and shamanic flavour. It is considered by many that the runes are divided into aettir ('aetts') as a kind of mnemonic device for an oral tradition, and this may well be one reason. But in addition I have also hinted at the pairing of the runes in dyads and the more mythic progression through the aett, such that it could be seen as outlining a creation mythology of the northern peoples, as well as a progression of the shamanic and magical influences. If this is true, we may well see that each aett tells a different story, although I would expect the magical input to be a continuous theme; after all, this is the prime 'purpose' of the runes!

And now to the second aett, that of Hagal:

ᚻ ᚺ

Hagal (Haegl)
Hail

Hail is the whitest of grain;
it is whirled from the vault of heaven
and is tossed about by gusts of wind
and then it melts into water.

It may be that the difference in the names represents one between the literal and metaphoric use of this rune, because **Haegl** may mean hail, but **Hagal** could also refer to a downfall or catastrophe. The rune implies this with the middle bars moving down between the two vertical staves (an alternative shape for **Hagal** in the Anglo-Saxon tradition has only one bar, like the Elder Futhark, and is often used interchangeably).

There are some similarities to **Ur** here, even in the shape, which reflects the primal ice of creation and indicates a creative function to **Hagal** in spite of its rather ominous obvious interpretation. In these respects **Hagal** also represents winter.

The creative function is indicated in the fact that all three rune poems refer to hail as grain, either as 'whitest' or 'cold/coldest' (Scandinavian rune poems). In the Old English poem there seems to be quite a longish description of this changing process, although the connection with 'heaven' is of spiritual interest, inferring that even in the darkness of winter – and the most severe inner catastrophe – there is a spiritual and shamanic component in operation.

Other rune rows often have a more clearly pictographic representation of hail as a six-sided star shape, like a snow flake (as with **Ior** in the Futhorc). The Old Norse poem refers to 'Christ created the world of old', which may refer to the creative and mythological aspect of hail, and 'Christ' being a later interpolation, or maybe in exchange for Odin/Woden? In the Icelandic poem the reference to hail as 'sickness of serpents' is enigmatic. Serpents appear on more than one occasion in the poems; it is tempting to read this phrase in a shamanic or tantric manner.

Hagal indicates that even in the worst adversity there is a creative potential that is spiritually inspired, and to 'stick it out'. This could be the sort of counsel given to someone with severe depression and to engage with the process creatively, rather than taking recourse to drugs to alleviate the suffering, which would only further block the creative and transformative process.

$\dagger$

Nyd
Need, Necessity

Trouble is oppressive to the heart;
yet often it proves a source of help
and salvation to the children of men,
to everyone who heeds it betimes.

An alternative name for **Nyd** is 'constraint', which the image implies with the crossing stave as a limit or blockage to the central stave. An alternative image is of two fire sticks, where the repeated friction of rubbing together ultimately leads to a fire. The term 'need-fire' is derived from this and sees conflict also as transition, as the need-fire was used for initiation rituals with the participant leaping through it. A lateral view is to see the image as the crossed-fingers of good luck.

By contrast the Scandinavian poems emphasise the constraint and oppressive aspects without the liberating aspect of the Old English poem. By now, this would seem a feature of the runes generally and makes me ask questions about the function and purpose of the Scandinavian poems: maybe the Christian influence is stronger than has been given credit and transcribed them in a more negative and repressive manner, thus – hopefully from that orientation – alienating the runes from the populace.

Nyd can also mean a knot, and here the Norns, or the three weavers of fate, can be seen as an association. **Nyd** is thus closely related with the enigmatic northern concept of 'wyrd'. In this respect 'betimes' may refer to the future, and hence taking on trouble as a transition to 'salvation'. In other words, if we avoid trouble (of the 'heart'), we may also miss a richer future.

Here, as elsewhere, the guidance is how to deal creatively, purposefully, and shamanically when mental turmoil is readily apparent. There is an accent in the runes (and hence in the times) of turmoil, trouble, and conflict, but the overwhelming attitude is one of acceptance of these forces as factors in our fate and personal evolution. This reinforces the concept of wyrd, or destiny, which is a profound influence for northern peoples.

Is

Ice

Ice is very cold and immeasurably slippery;
it glistens as clear as glass and most like to gems;
it is a floor wrought by the frost, fair to look upon.

The image here, somewhat like an icicle, is self-evident. The poem describes some of the dangers (cold, slippery) and also some of the beauty (gems, fair to look upon) that are inherent in the danger. This all indicates the strange and paradoxical attraction that danger may hold for us and is represented by **Is**: Fear and excitement can form a paradoxical pair.

The floor is something to be crossed, and the Norse poem refers to it as a 'broad bridge'. The poem goes on to say that 'the blind man must be led', indicating that crossing is a necessity or fate requiring assistance. But with the 'blind man', who or what does the leading? Mythologically the 'blind man' has an 'inner' sight; that is, of and through the 'third eye'. Although tangential, the bridge that connects the everyday world, Midgard, with Asgard (the realm of the gods) is called 'bifrost'. There is no direct literal connection here with the 'wrought by the frost' mentioned above, or the frequent references to frost in the poems, because bifrost is a 'firey' bridge and likened to the rainbow, yet I still find the association interesting and intriguing.

In a psychological sense ice can be enchanting and cause us to become stuck; there is frequent mythological reference to this, mainly in fairy stories, particularly if involving the 'Ice Queen'. The Icelandic poem even refers to the 'destruction of the doomed', doom being a more sinister aspect of fate (or wyrd), and more like the term 'fatal'. It is as if we must beware of becoming entranced, or fixed, by forces that seem beautiful and enchanting. It is also that we may need other forces to 'lead' us (as a blinded or 'blind man') from this state; a hint of a deeper spiritual reality as exemplified by bifrost and the Norse rune poem.

The reference to fate, wyrd, and doom recalls the comments around **Nyd**. If **Nyd** represents one of the Norns (the female weavers of fate) and the future, then **Is** would represent the Norn of the present. Then where is the Norn of the past? The closest association may well be **Hagal** and, if so, these three runes can be seen to form a functional unity, which they seem to be in both image and tone.

Additionally the order past, future, present is at variance to our linear concept of time of being past > present > future, which itself is worthy of contemplation.

Ger

Year, Harvest

Summer is a joy to men, when God, the holy King of heaven,
suffers the earth to bring forth shining fruits
for rich and poor alike.

The association with the year appears present in the central part of the image. In the Elder Futhark this central image, minus the stave, is split lengthways and separated a little vertically, so that it looks like a **Kenaz** rune with its mirror image circling each other, as do the seasons. This is the two halves of the year, such that **Ger** represents the whole year, even though the poem calls it summer.

In the north the year began with the coming of winter rather than the summer, as is still recognised in the yearly cycle of the Northern Hemisphere. (Traditionally also, the dusk or night marks the beginning of the next day.) So summer is the culmination of the year and its bountifulness, with the continuing theme of spiritual equality ('rich and poor alike'). The emphasis here is strongly on the agricultural cycle and its variations.

Both the Scandinavian poems use the word 'boon' here, and neither have the seemingly strong Christian message, which stands in a paradoxical contrast to my comments in the **Nyd** rune (above). However, this may all simply represent the mixing of cultures and ideologies over place and time, as there are many such paradoxes in the rune material we have to hand. In this particular rune the Christian message is loud and clear, even to the use of the word 'suffers'. It may be that 'God, the holy King of heaven' replaces a pagan identity here.

Ger represents plenty, as well as our profound connection to the earth we live on and indirectly to our bodies, and the welfare of both, which are ultimately deeply connected. Phonetically, this rune is connected in the Younger Futhark by **Ar** to **Ass/Os** and hence the god Woden, who may be the god that the 'holy King of heaven' has replaced in the Old English poem.

ᛇ

Eoh
Yew (tree)

The yew is a tree with a rough bark,
hard and fast in the earth, supported by its roots,
a guardian of flame and a joy upon an estate.

Here – and in the next two runes – the Old English rune poem has no Scandinavian equivalent in this position of the Futhorc, yet it does appear as the final rune of the Younger Futhark as **Yr** (combining **Eoh** with **Eolh**, the 15th rune), using a shape that is an inverted **Eolh**. These manipulations reflect much of the evolving phonetics of each language, particularly the vowels, which can be an additional point of confusion that I am attempting to minimise here.

We will also come across the yew again when we move to the additional runes of the Old English Futhorc, although there is a differentiation here between the tree as yew and its common usage as a bow, whereas in the Scandinavian rune poems the two aspects stand side-by-side in the **Yr** rune.

The associations with the yew tree in northern cultures are invariably positive, making their connection with graveyards (and hence death) interesting. This may reflect that Churches were often built on existing sacred areas of the pagan peoples they supervened, whose attitude to death was by no means as pessimistic, thus effecting a further level of psychological and social control.

The yew is the oldest and strongest of trees, and can live up to 2,000 years. Its strength is one reason it is used for the making of bows, as well as being durable for fires ('guardian of flame'). This strength is reflected in the image, which is not unlike the backbone or spine of man.

Eoh reflects strength, durability, and resilience. The connection with the earth and support of the roots would reinforce this, but in northern cultures it also reflects the connection to our heritage and the ancestors.

Peorth
A Game

Peorth is a source of recreation and amusement to the great,
where warriors sit blithely together in the banqueting-hall.

The meaning of this rune is problematic, and we do not have recourse to the Scandinavian poems for help. If the pairing aspect of the runes is considered, then as **Eoh** represents the yew tree it could be postulated that this **Peorth** may represent a tree as well, maybe a deciduous one because of its shape.

However, this shape could represent other things, such as a gaming-cup (for dice etc.), or even a womb. The last will have more significance when we come to **Beorc**, and **Peorth** then seen as an 'open' representation of that rune. The impression of a womb or creative container is strong, and reminiscent of the athanor of alchemy; the container into which the base material for change is placed, to be 'worked on' by the attendant alchemist as a metaphor for his or her own personal and spiritual transformation.

The overall impression here is fruitfulness and change. This is reflected in the 'gaming' association, which is indicative of chance and luck, hence the flux of life and once again change. The word 'blithely' indicates a casual indifference, something northern warriors were renowned for in battle. If they died in battle they were transported to the great banqueting-hall of Valhalla, assisted by the Valkyries, and this may represent a level of kenning also present in the **Peorth** rune.

The overall impression is of change and the flux of life. In this respect the connection to the concept of wyrd is profound, accepting what we are 'given' and 'making the most of it' in the colloquial but also the spiritual sense. A challenge to the soul and our personal development seems inherent in **Peorth**.

Eolh
Protection, Elk-sedge

The Eolh-sedge is mostly to be found in a marsh;
it grows in the water and makes a ghastly wound,
covering with blood every warrior who touches it.

Although there is no direct Scandinavian representation of **Eolh** in the other poems, the rune shape is used for the **Man** rune of the Younger Futhark, where the 20th **Man** rune of the Futhorc/Elder Futhark is also incorporated. This is hardly surprising, as the shape strongly suggests a man with arms raised, or even the splaying of the first three fingers of the hand; one an act of supplication, the other more of protection.

The act of supplication, in the religious sense, is not emphasised in the rune poem, although the word 'augmentation' is used in both versions of the Scandinavian poems related to **Man**. I think this aspect has been somewhat overlooked, and see this rune to also be one of prayer and dedication. It is certainly energetically powerful to stand with arms raised in an evocative posture and in the manner of the rune – try it.

But the rune poem says otherwise. Here, as is a general feature of the Futhorc, **Eolh** is reduced to a literal and somewhat floral perspective. Certainly the elk-sedge is a sharp plant that grows in marshland and can inflict a wound if grasped. One extension of this is seeing the elk-sedge as a boundary plant, not unlike a hedge, and often symbolising the marginal or liminal existence of the magician who lives in the world beyond and which the hedge affords protection for. This being the case, the 'blood' of the 'warrior' may have a shamanic and initiatory significance.

However, the elk as animal is ignored, and probably overlaps its magical kenning as a shamanistic 'power animal'. Closely connected to the horse in northern culture and having regal and spiritual significance (particularly if the horned stag – the horned god – is considered), the elk is an animal that in the wild seems to walk the boundary between the physical and spiritual worlds. It therefore affords a protection of a different but overlapping kind.

ᛋ

Sigel
Sun

The sun is ever a joy in the hopes of seafarers
when the journey away over the fishes' bath,
until the courser of the deep bears them to land.

All rune poems refer directly or indirectly to the sun – but not the moon – and in an obvious manner. The image could be seen as a ray of the sun and, when doubled, is known as a svastica (or swastika) of Indo-European descent, meaning 'to be good'. As we know, the National Socialist Party, or Nazi movement, of the 20th century, inverted this meaning.

The power of the sun is identified in the Norse ('I bow to the divine decree') and Icelandic poems ('destroyer of ice'). The sun had significance in the north and often had a feminine attribute (possibly most specifically to the goddess Freo, as amber was seen as the 'tears of the sun', and refers symbolically to her tears), which is understandable when the extreme cycles of the sun are experienced the more north one ventures, where the cyclic variation of the sun is more pronounced.

In the poem above the indication is that the sun was an important feature to the seafaring peoples of the north ('the fishes' bath' is a metaphor for the sea), particularly when it is considered how far they ventured and expanded prior to Christianisation. The 'courser of the deep' may refer to a horse and journey, as exemplified in both earlier and later runes in the Futhorc, but also metaphorically points to spiritual assistance on life's journey.

The sun indicates not only the spiritual world, but also to its manifestation within this world without recourse to any interme-diary god or goddesses; that is, apart from the consideration of Freo (and she indirectly). In modern language **Sigel** is a direct connection with the higher self. The name itself may also refer to a 'sigil', being an inscribed symbol having magical power, which is how this rune symbol is often used in the form of an amulet.

The Hagal aett as a whole seems to fall into two equal parts. The first four runes appear to be a continuation of the creative process of the first aett, although much more on the human plane. Then there seems a change in tone, marked by **Ger**. Although a modern interpretation, I have found it of interest to assign each of the first twelve runes to a month, starting with **Feoh** coming after winter. The aettir also lend themselves to a more traditional eightfold manifestation around the yearly cycle, which has ceremonial significance. There are many other permutations and combinations, which you may like to experiment with.

My sense is that this aett is one of individual creation, manifestation, and an evolution that extends to the following – Tir's – aett. The first three runes, being an extension of the first aett, seem to define an individual's existence. Then there is a progression of conception to birth and coming into existence as the 'higher self' that will make the next aett interesting reading.

Now to Tir's aett:

↑

Tir
The God

Tiw is a guiding star; well does it keep faith with princes;
it is ever on its course over the mists of night and never fails.

The rune **Tir** – here in the rune poem designated as **Tiw**, an alternative spelling – represents the god who lost a hand to the wolf Fenrir, a monstrous animal that threatened all of mankind (as well as the gods). The loss was a consequence of the trade-off that kept Fenrir chained, and therefore not a threat to the peace and tranquillity of the Aesir (gods), as well as indicating Tir's role in justice. You may want the check out the myth to see how he ultimately lost his hand!

Tir is referred to as the 'one-handed god' in both Scandinavian poems, indicating again the more profound mythological connections existing in those cultures. With Thor and Woden/Odin he is one of the 'big three' of the northern pantheon.

Tir is a sky god as indicated in the poem, and, rather like Uranus and his usurper, Zeus, in Greek mythology, Woden ultimately superseded him during the 'migration age' (800 CE – 1100 CE). Both are gods of war, although Woden adopted this with his other functions, leaving Tir as the god of justice. The runic image does seem to lend itself to phallic interpretation, although this does not appear a distinct feature of the god; like Zeus, this sexual aspect was more the province of Woden.

As a sky god, **Tir** would seem primordial, though in our time he presents a more humanised face, which is a characteristic of his aett. As the rune poem indicates, he is the god of justice, predictability, and order. From an inner perspective this implies honesty and integrity, the moral imperative in man.

Tiw is the alternative rendering of **Tir**, resonating phonetically in our 'Tuesday'. Similarly Wednesday is Woden's day, Thursday Thor's day, and Friday could be Frey's day... or maybe Freo's day if we are being democratic!

Beorc
Birch

The poplar bears no fruit; yet without seed it brings forth suckers,
for it is generated from its leaves.
Splendid are its branches and gloriously adorned
its lofty crown that reaches to the skies.

Although the reference here is to the poplar and is supported botanically, all the imagery points to the birch. It is fertile, vigorous and plentiful, and the reference to 'skies' may associate it with **Tir**.

The fertility is implied in the image itself, which is distinctly feminine, whichever way you look at it. This shows a further level of complementarity to **Tir**: god and goddess, sky and earth, male and female. The sexual imagery is deeply embedded here and not to be ignored, although in **Beorc** this is woman and all her power. Reference has been made to a possible association to **Peorth**, which further reinforces this interpretation.

However, the reference in the rune poem is to 'self generation' and is implied in the imagery. There is a sense of spring and abundance, and of a tree reaching up to the sky. The almost cosmic imagery is further supported by reference to the 'lofty crown', which paints a regal picture.

The Scandinavian poems do not have the richness and abundance of the Old English poem, which may indicate a climatic difference and the relative richness of the British Isles. In the Old Norse poem the reference to 'Loki was fortunate in his deceit' is very enigmatic, which I wonder about in reference to the different trees implied in this rune, which also includes the fir. Loki is the master trickster, maybe pointing to a level of kenning not yet appreciated in the rune.

All this notwithstanding, **Beorc** is about deep and self-contained feminine energy that is capable of regal appearance and aspiration, even to reaching the sky. This energy is subtle, contained, and yet also strong.

M

Eh

Horse

The horse is a joy to princes in the presence of warriors.
A steed in the pride of its hoofs,
when rich men on horseback bandy words about it;
and it is ever a source of comfort to the restless.

The horse has been touched on in several places to date. In this **Eh** rune the relationship between the horse and its rider is funda-mental, and even symbolised within the image itself. In fact, relationship itself is embodied in this rune, which could be seen as two horses nuzzling noses, or a couple walking hand-in-hand. Without doubt this man-horse relationship was of historic and military significance, and hence its importance, being a feature of Indo-European peoples. It should be recalled that the fantasy image of the centaur is derived from this close relationship, possibly by observers who – unused to riders on horses – saw the two so interconnected as to be one being.

Yet there are levels beyond the literal, as the horse represents power and the relationship to it that is not seen with other animals in the runes. To harness the power of the horse requires a delicate balance between the rider and steed, which may add another level of kenning to 'princes' and 'rich men'. In this respect the horse could represent not only the body, but also be a symbol of the soul.

In shamanism the soul of the shaman often explores the 'otherworld' in the guise of a 'power animal', often unique to the individual shaman. Of course, this need not be a horse, but the horse is a strong image of this relationship and the journey that is to be undertaken by the shaman. It should be recalled that Woden had an eight-legged horse, Sleipnir, upon which he traversed the 'worlds' in a vertical (spiritual) rather than in a linear (physical) manner.

Of further interest, mythologically, shamanically and enigmatically, is that Sleipnir is the product of the 'union' of Loki – in the form of a mare – with a stallion. The myth involves the building of the walls to protect Asgard, the home of the Aesir, and is worth checking out.

As the horse **Eh** represents our power at different levels and involves a differing concept of control; it is more one based on co-operation with the unknown or spiritual dimensions. Too much control and we can 'kill the spirit' of the animal, too little and it can run amok; it would seem to be all in the balance. There are obvious similarities to **Rad** here.

ᛗ

Man
Man

The joyous man is dear to his kinsman;
yet every man is doomed to fail his fellow,
since the Lord by his decree will commit the vile carrion to the earth.

Together with the **Eh** rune, the **Man** rune would seem to create another dyad. As **Eh** could even be seen as two **Lagu** runes (the rune coming next) facing each other, the same could be said of **Man** with a doubling of the **Wyn** rune. This may be reflected in the first line, which reinforces man's divine connection, but does not continue through the poem, which in all sources indicates his mortality.

The paradox continues in the Scandinavian poems that, whilst reinforcing man's mortality, also see him as the 'adorner of ships' in the Icelandic (recall the longboats of the Vikings) and the 'claw' of the 'hawk' in the Norse ('great is the claw of the hawk'). Although this latter reference could indicate his mortality, it may have a shamanic reference; it is also the only place in the immediate rune literature where a bird is mentioned, until we get to the extended version of the Futhorc, which I find of unexplained interest. Of further interest is that the **Man** rune is graphically represented by the **Eolh** rune in the Younger Futhark.

The Old English rune poem is – again – laden with Christian reference, with 'vile' indicating not only man's deprecated status, but also his potentially inherent evil nature (after all, evil is an anagram of vile). There is also the word 'doom' used again; in this context it is an indication of man's mortality, his impending death.

All in all **Man** is a representation of exactly that, man in his totality (I use the word man here to include woman and, indeed, the image verifies this sexual duality), with his connection to the gods, but also his fragility and mortality. We are a unique composite standing between the worlds, as is readily seen in the mythology of all peoples and reflected in our psychophysical totality of body and mind.

Ϝ

Lagu
Lake

The ocean seems interminable to men,
if they continue on the rolling bark
and the waves of the sea terrify them
and the courser of the deep heed not its bridle.

Here is the half of the **Eh** rune described above, reinforced by the 'courser of the deep', with the word 'bridle' confirming that this phrase represents a horse, a symbolic 'sea-horse'. By contrast, and maybe without the connection to the **Eh** rune, the Scandinavian poems seem gentle and even innocuous. Only the Norse poem provides some symbolic depth with a 'waterfall' and 'ornaments are of gold', which may refer to the 'tears of the land' and the complement of amber; it would also connect this rune with Freo and the feminine.

The 'bark' reference comes up in the **Iss** (Ice) rune of the Icelandic poem, with 'bark of rivers' and even 'roof of the wave', indicating bark in this context to be the froth and foam of the wave. Whilst bark could refer to a tree (indeed, one dictionary definition relates it directly to **Beorc**) it could also indicate the noise, as in the bark of a dog, that is made by the waves.

Overall the English poem provides a challenging, even terrifying view of the ocean. In the poem this is particularly so if the courser 'heed not its bridle' and indicating, once again, the dynamic balance existent in nature and man's role within it. This does, of course, and as already discussed, reinforce man's role in this balance: although in this image he would seem to be at the mercy of the elements.

Although not directly referenced in the poems, the word 'lagu' is related to the Germanic word for leek. With garlic and onion, this plant was considered to have magical properties; indeed they are all generally considered to have strong and pervasive healing qualities. Additionally, the leek, as with the image itself, has a strong phallic appearance. This is seemingly at odds with the image as sea, lake, and hence the feminine. However, there may be other associations here that enforce a more complex sexual symbolism.

Specifically from a magical perspective, the sea, lake and water represent the maternal matrix, or the womb. The lady of the lake is an image from Celtic spirituality that reinforces this image, and provides a complex and even sexual symbolism for the casting of Excalibur. Magicians, more specifically witches, also use water for divinatory scrying.

Lagu is the deep feminine in her mythological, magical, and archetypal context, beyond the simplicity of the mother's womb. The images are wide and complex, sexual and mystical, but overall – and with the association of Freo – point to the Vanir and the magic of seith.

Ing
The God (or Frey)

Ing was first seen by men among the East-Danes;
till, followed by his chariot, he departed eastwards over the waves.
So the Heardingas named the hero.

Ing is an ancient god of the land, rather than the earth per se (a feminine function), and may be paired with **Lagu** as land-water. This would also associate the god Ing with Freo, which occurs in other myths in his guise as Frey. Ing is fundamentally a fertility god, as is Frey in his pairing with Freo, with all the attendant sexual implications.

The image can be seen in several ways. As an enclosure it indicates containment as of a race or people. As a seed it is fertility, both of semen and the egg, particularly with the association to Ing and Frey, and hence Freo. In the rune rows it is also a seed, as its shape manifests in a lot of the runes.

One variation of **Ing** extends the lines at the top and bottom of the rune making it a reflective doubling of the **Kenaz** rune of the Elder Futhorc. In this form it is also a doubling of **Gyfu**, thus reinforcing the meanings associated with that rune. Turned 90 degrees to the right it could be a pictograph of a couple making love, viewed from below.

The Ingvaeones, one of the core Germanic tribes involved in the Anglo-Saxon migrations, also lived close to the sea. The East-Danes could be the Swedes. The chariot is an image that often refers to the skies and maybe a constellation of stars. The Heardingas are a royal line of East Anglia. Whilst these associations expand on the rune poem with a historical flavour, I am not sure whether they add much in terms of magical meaning.

Instead we can return to the prior comments, where the rune

is the fertility of the land and represents a seed, even semen. Separately, and in combination with **Lagu**, there is a lot of encoded imagery that relates to seith magic, but also the fertility of the land in the agricultural cycle.

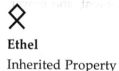

Ethel
Inherited Property

An estate is very dear to every man,
if he can enjoy there in his house
whatever is right and proper in constant prosperity

Ethel and the rune that follows, **Daeg**, seem somewhat interchangeable in their relative positions at the end of the Germanic and Scandinavian Futharks. There are arguments for and against what the order should be, as would be expected with such a variation (existent nowhere else in these Futharks). Here I will simply adopt the order as given in the Old English rune poem, and do not enter into the argument. As neither is represented in the Scandinavian rune poems, these cannot be drawn upon for assistance.

There is general agreement as to the meaning of this rune in the common and literal sense. Having pictographic and ideological similarities to **Ing**, it represents not only individual land or estate, but also tribal lands, and extends to the idea of heritage across generations. In this sense the rune image can be seen to be a boundary, a fencing of owned land.

All this, of course, can also be a metaphor or metaphors for the individual in an inner manner. In other words it relates to genetic heritage, ancestry, and its manifestation in the world. In this respect the image is like a man (many of them are, you may have noticed) in a balanced posture. The idea of a boundary is also relevant, in a relative manner, to how a man conducts himself in the world. The term 'right and proper' and the word 'prosperity' link the **Ethel** rune to others in the Futhorc.

An additional image is of a ring, symbol of inheritance, kinship, or even kingship. An archetypal symbol of the self, the ring is a powerful image of ownership, containment, and power.

ᛞ

Daeg
Day

Day, the glorious light of the Creator, is sent by the Lord;
it is beloved of men, a source of hope and happiness to rich and poor,
and of service to all.

Whilst the **Daeg** rune is commonly represented as two right-angled triangles facing each other nose-to-nose, the image represents day as 'day-night' and the cyclic flow between the two. Indeed, this may be a hidden or lost feature of other runes, such as **Sigel** (sun-moon) and **Ger** (summer-winter), in that each name latently and paradoxically contains its opposite. An alternative version extends the two vertical staves in both directions. This then makes **Daeg** look like two facing **Thorns**, or even **Man** with a little slippage in the middle.

There is little in the literal sense here, and the Christianisation I hope you can now recognise as being particularly strong. As elsewhere, I often wonder what is hidden or excluded in this process. In the absence of natural or agricultural reference, the rune would seem to refer more to the day as 'light' in the spiritual sense. That the image inherently contains the opposite ('darkness') is of particular interest in this Christianisation process, which has totally excluded it.

However, all this does not stop the spiritual connotation of light being of divine origin and the great leveller; that is, it can bring 'hope and happiness to rich and poor'. Also inherent in the poem is the **Sigel** or Sun rune, which closes this aett on a light and spiritual note similar to the preceding one of **Hagal**.

The third aett has a much lighter quality than the second, particularly the first half starting with **Hagal**. In some ways this supports the theme of the Futhorc to date (and in the Elder Futhark) being divided into two sequences of twelve, as the last four runes of the **Hagal** aett connect with the **Tir** aett in a similar manner to the first four connecting to the **Feoh** aett. Anyway, this is speculative; certainly there was a great emphasis on 'eight' in the north, being the way the year and its attendant ceremonies were divided, but I suspect there is a significance in the twelve as well.

Certainly the **Tir** aett is more related to man and his relationship to the land and earth. However, the magical and spiritual elements are metaphorically (at least) present in all the runes, as well as permeating the Futhorc to date as a whole. It will now be of interest to see how these insights flow into the extended Futhorc, with restricted guidance from the Old English rune poem, and now with more emphasis on our own individual insights and associations.

The Rune Extension

Runes 25 – 33

The extension of the Futhorc was probably to deal with phonetic developments in language by the Anglo-Saxons in their new homeland, prior to the wholesale adoption of the Roman alphabet there.

As stated earlier, I have generally avoided substantial reference to the phonetic development of the runes. At the most immediate level this is because I believe there is too much emphasis on trying to relate – or even equate – the Futhorc to the use of the Roman script. That this can be done, to a relative sense of completion, there can be no doubt. But this does not equate the two and gives the erroneous impression that the Futhorc in some way is simply a language that can be equally well, or even better, expressed through Roman script, and therefore more easily understood.

My concern here is that this diminishes the other dimensions to the Futhorc; being the metaphoric, symbolic, imaginative, magical, and spiritual dimensions, which are progressively reduced in the Roman script and almost completely absent in modern English, in an overt context (I contend they are still present covertly to a greater or lesser extent). Seeing the runes in their own light facilitates this process, because even the scholarly material does not point to such a conflation of the two; in fact, it does the opposite and is one reason this direction is not explored.

All these comments notwithstanding, the initial extension to the Futhorc – the first 5 runes – was primarily phonetic and therefore trying to accommodate language changes and development. It may also be that these runes reflect some sort of synthesis between the indigenous and migrating Anglo-Saxon cultures.

It is here, maybe, that the Futhorc parts company with the more esoteric trends in the Elder Futhark, as represented and reinforced by the development of the Younger Futhark. In this earlier stage (around 500 CE) it may be that the Futhorc was seen as a written language before being superseded by the Roman script. This later development of the Younger Futhark in the Viking era, several hundred years later, may then be seen as some sort of return to a magical authenticity.

Following the change in the phonetic meaning of the **Os** rune (where the 4th rune of the Elder Futhark becomes the 26th of the Futhorc, which with the variation in the 6th **Cen** rune together accounts for the name change from Futhark to Futhorc), these changes were to accommodate the varied vowel usage and being a, ae, y and ea. These are present in the inscription of the Futhorc on the so-called Thames seax (a 9th century knife found in the River Thames in 1857), although the rune poem brings in io/ia – a slightly enigmatic rune, as we shall see – between y and ea. The last four runes (30 to 33) are consonants that rarely occur in inscriptions, but are present in manuscripts. These are collectively called the Northumbrian rune row that originated around 800 CE, and which has a mythic or symbolic significance that indicates a reconnection to an evolving and ongoing uniquely spiritual development in England. This is in quite a different manner to the Elder Futhark's contraction into the Younger Futhark, as well as the actual spiritual content and orientation.

As before, I will leave further research of the phonetic aspects of the runes to individual pursuit, as they take this exploration in a direction largely incommensurate with the magical and spiritual usage I am espousing.

This ongoing sequence is sometimes referred to as the fourth aett:

ᚪ

Ac
Oak

The oak fattens the flesh of pigs for the children of men.
Often it traverses the gannet's bath,
and the ocean proves whether the oak keeps faith
in honourable fashion.

The clear meaning here of **Ac** is of the oak tree, strong and hardy. The two principle uses of oak were of its fruit, the acorn, for pig food, and as the most resilient wood for the building of ships, so vital to the seafaring Germanic peoples. This would have related to those peoples of the south and west, including the British Isles, as the oak does not grow in places like Iceland and the extreme north of Scandinavia. The rune poem contains only the second bird reference, although it is metaphoric; here it is 'gannet's bath' for the sea, seemingly in preference to 'fishes' bath' as mentioned earlier in the **Sigel** rune.

The image is a slightly truncated **Os** rune, which connects it to the gods, although more specifically to Thor with the strength and power of the oak. The oak has a magical quality that is revered amongst the Celtic peoples and their priesthood, the Druids, the religion that the Anglo-Saxons usurped.

In these respects, and from a more magical perspective, the **Ac** rune represents power, and specifically power of the magical will. Symbolically, the image is of a man holding a stick or wand, as would a magician. This is reinforced by other features common to the oak, such as being steadfast, resilient, and coura-geous – all features of the good magician.

Ac calls for strength and endurance, and complements the **Ur** rune in many ways. As such it is a rune of healing; dealing with the projections of others in a creative and magical manner. From this perspective **Ac** relates more to Woden and a different spiritual perspective to that of Thor.

ᚫ

Aesc
Ash

The ash is exceedingly high and precious to men.
With its sturdy trunk it offers a stubborn resistance,
though attacked by many a man.

This 26th rune of the Futhorc has taken on the symbolic image of the 4th rune of the Elder Futhark, **Ass**. Indirectly, **Aesc** has taken on some of **Ass's** characteristics with the latter's change from the Elder Futhark to **Os** in the Futhorc. The ash tree is characteristically that of Odin/Woden, as it was on the ash, which may have been the world tree Yggdrasil, where he hung for nine days and nights in his shamanic discovery of the runes in the well of Mimir, with the subsequent gaining of their attendant wisdom.

The similarity to oak is indicated in the shape and its commonality of the rune shapes, as well as the closeness phonetically. In the poem these common features continue, although 'attack' is a little unclear. If the ash represents Yggdrasil, the world-tree of Norse mythology, then it is under attack from its roots being perpetually eaten by the 'worms' that gnaw at its roots.

The meaning of this rune overlaps that of **Ac** considerably, although the mythological associations to Germanic mythology remain quite strong. The ash is also synonymous with the making of spears rather than bows, a fact that has considerable association with ritual sacrifice, and was a feature of Odin/Woden's self-sacrifice.

With the conflation of these runes across the Futharks, and within the Futhorc itself, it is difficult to see **Aesc** in isolation. There is also some association symbolically with the **Eh** rune, although there it is a yew tree. However, it does appear in the next rune. In fact, it is worth seeing these three runes in some sort of continuum and maybe, as discussed a little earlier, indicating a convergence of ideas with the indigenous spirituality that the Anglo-Saxons met on their arrival in England.

ᛁ᛫

Yr

Yew bow

Yr is a source of joy and honour to every prince and knight;
it looks well on a horse and is reliable equipment for a journey.

Yr is yet another tree rune, reinforcing their importance in the Futhorc as compared to the Futhark. The yew is represented in the 13th rune of the Futhorc, **Eoh**, but the difference here is the reference to its use as a bow, which it pictographically resembles. The yew rune of the same name in the Younger Futhark, the 16th and last, makes combined reference to the tree, bow, and arrow.

The first line of the poem indicates its significance with 'joy and honour', whilst the second line associates with two other images and known runes, being the horse and the journey (**Eh** and **Rad**).

The bow and arrow is reliable equipment to take on a journey and for use in hunting; its use possibly precedes even the origin of the runes. It is also able to have an impact over a long distance, which may be its symbolic and magical relevance, in addition to its use as a weapon.

Of further interest is that the pictorial image is of the **Ur** rune with an arrow inside, so the attributes of **Ur** would also be relevant here.

I tend to see a relative distinction between the above three runes from the two that follow; the reason for this I trust will become apparent as we progress:

IOR (or IAR)

Fish, Eel or Serpent

Iar is a river fish and yet it always feeds on land;
it has a fair abode encompassed by water, where it lives in happiness.

This is a strange beast, literally as well as symbolically. Literally the meaning of **Ior/Iar** is uncertain: a 'river fish' that 'feeds on land'? It is apparent that an eel may well fit the bill, but it is by no means clear that this is the case.

From the symbolic perspective, backed by the rune poem as well as some etymological gymnastics, I would favour **Ior** meaning a serpent, even a sea-serpent. Serpents, worms and dragons abound in Germanic mythology; and the rune image, although with a striking resemblance to the Younger Futhark **Hagall** (hail) rune, looks serpentine enough to me.

If this is the case, then this rune is slightly out of context with the three before, and the one that follows, that make up the 29 runes of the poem. Maybe, in this case (and as some commentators think) it should follow the next rune **Ear** and bridge to the more mythic Northumbrian extension to 33 runes.

In the magical context the serpent is a strong sexual image that recalls the kundalini energy coiled at the base of the spine, evoked and awakened by ritual sexual activity. It is a – if not the – primal energetic power in the human psychophysical organism. There is a sense here of balance and gender equality, with the gender-ambiguous nature of the serpent. Yet the serpent, or snake as kundalini, is the primal force of our spiritual evolution where the male and female elements are also in balance. This may be the prime feature of **Ior**, balance in the primal sense, as reinforced by its home in the waters of the planetary maternal womb.

Ear

Earth, soil

The grave is horrible to every knight,
when the corpse quickly begins to cool
and is laid in the bosom of the dark earth.
Prosperity declines, happiness passes away
and covenants are broken.

With the possible exception of **Ior**, and if the Thames seax is considered, **Ear** is the final rune of the Futhorc as defined by the rune poem. It therefore represents finality, with some degree of dark imagery and pessimism: it is not a cheerful rune. With it, the body passes away and disorder once again supervenes.

However, the decay is not just physical in the poem, it is also mental, emotional, and social; it cuts across a wide spectrum of meaning. Although seemingly related to personal death, the images also recall the mythic Ragnarok, the 'twilight of the gods', where everything passes away and anticipates a new beginning. In this there are some remarkable similarities, as with Woden's self-sacrifice, with Christian belief.

This is not a rapid death, it is one of decomposition, and reminds us of the alchemical stages of putrefaction and fermentation. These stages mark the transition between the consolidation of the soul in the 'lesser work' with its transition to the spiritual 'greater work'. In this respect **Ior** has distinct parallels to the crucifixion and resurrection; indeed the image could be a man suspended on a cross. If so, and my intuition is correct, this rune marks a transition into these latter runes of the Futhorc, which contain a merging with the mystical aspects of the Christian influence.

This marks the end of the Old English rune poem and most extant versions of the Futhorc. However, there are four further runes, derived from what is known as the Northumbrian rune row and usually preserved in manuscript form, that are particularly worth considering:

Cweorth
Ritual fire

Cweorth is the ritual fire of change and transformation. It complements **Nyd** in many ways, although here it is more as the receptacle of the fire initiated in **Nyd**. The image is of the flames leaping up into the air. As cremation, it is the liberation of the spirit from the body. In ritual initiation, and as commenced in **Nyd**, it is the completion, the transformation. In many ways this is an extension of **Nyd** in terms of process, yet also and more particularly that of **Ear**.

Of further interest here is that the rune image is of **Peorth**, with the lower stave a mirror image of that rune. The name is similar and even complementary; phonetically it is 'p' and 'q' respectively. This may provide insight into the **Peorth** rune; is it a fire container, an oven, or an alchemical athanor (vessel)?

In alchemy, the prima materia, the base material to be transformed, is placed in a container called an athanor, as we have discussed elsewhere. Then heat is applied and the process of transformation initiated. Is this the next stage from the somewhat alchemically flavoured death of **Ear**? Is this alchemical process mirrored in the runes **Peorth** and **Cweorth**?

I think there is more to be considered here with these questions. **Cweorth** indicates a process of change or transition that succeeds **Ear**. It is clearly delineated in the alchemical process and indicates a difficult but life-changing transition that demands support rather than protection from these forces. It is a powerful image that, to my mind, reinforces much of the pathways of spiritual evolution that are symbolised in the crucifixion and resurrection, and hence reinforcing the progressive Christian influence in these latter runes.

Calc
Cup, Chalice

Obviously **Calc** is an inverted **Eolh** rune, the 15th of the Futhorc and Elder Futhark. In the Younger Futhark there is a direct correlation with the 16th and last rune, **Yr**, the yew bow. As this 16th rune marks the end of the Younger Futhark, it can relate to death. Obviously, as can be seen above, the **Yr** of the Younger Futhark becomes rune 27 of the Futhorc and takes a different shape, akin to **Ur**. Although seemingly a little confusing to our modern and rational consciousness, this 'cross-fertilisation' between the various rune patterns indicates a dynamic interchange at various levels of kenning, also seen elsewhere.

There are resonances of the death association here with the inversion of the cup image, and the chalice association portends the death of Jesus, as well as the mystery of the Eucharist. In this respect the more mystical stream of Christianity via the Holy Grail is hinted at. Some commentators even picture **Calc** inverted, not unlike an upright chalice.

In all these connections death is not a final act, but a transformation. In the Germanic tradition the drinking horn would serve a social and religious function, as well, and parallels much of the Christian imagery. Here are points of merging and connection that indicate a creative flowing together of imagery and symbolism in these changing times, at least at a spiritual level, rather than seeing them as fundamentally adversarial as we are so often taught.

Although I have hinted at the connection between the previous rune, **Cweorth**, and **Peorth** in the second aett as an alchemical container, it may be that this is the function of **Calc**. Being adjacent to **Cweorth** and with the dyadic theme that permeates the Futhorc, this is an additional possibility. However, there is also the sense that this is of a higher order of transition or spiritual evolution.

One interesting observation here is the simple fact that **Calc** is actually an inverted **Eolh**. This inversion peculiarity is seen here in the Futhorc and the Younger Futhark, indicating that the modern habit of identifying a different meaning in readings where runes are 'inverted' would not have been a traditional one. This particular 'inversion' may have been of more magical and mystical import.

Stan
Stone

Stan is a familiar term in the Anglo-Saxon world and persists in male and family names. The wider association to stone is indicative of stability and a grounded quality, which the image itself presents. Indeed, it could be a rune stone itself, or symbolise the use of stones for inscriptions. It may also hark back to the Stone Age and the heritage from there that flows through the Futhorc.

The image could also be seen as an enclosed **Peorth**, adding another level of mystery to that rune and its possible further connection with these latter runes of the Futhorc. Certainly there is a sense of 'potential energy' within the image with all these associations.

Continuing the alchemical theme is the concept of the 'stone of the philosopher', which is the base material – the prima materia – and is the beginning of the 'work' to become the 'philosopher's stone' – a somewhat confusing and paradoxical terminology that reinforces alchemy's reputation as being somewhat obfuscatory. This resultant philosopher's stone is believed to catalyse the transformation of base metals into gold, as well as being the 'elixir of life'.

This latter association provides a connection of **Stan** with **Calc** and the Holy Grail, as well as the ultimate outcome of the alchemical process.

The final 33rd rune could be considered part of the fourth aett, or on its own:

Gar
Spear

Mythologically the spear is that of Woden and is representative of Yggdrasil, the world-tree; it is also the spear that is part of Woden's self-sacrifice to obtain galdor, the wisdom of the 'word' contained in the runes. This, as well as the image itself, tends to mark **Gar** apart from the other runes that precede it, although it remains symbolically connected.

Gar is somewhat enigmatic as well as being complex. It has no direct associations, particularly phonetically – 'g' is, after all, the **Gyfu** rune. From the Christian perspective, the spear used as part of Jesus' sacrifice also comes to mind and illustrates that this may be a rune of self-sacrifice. Psychologically it may represent the death of the 'ego', but in spiritual or alchemical terminology it may be the ultimate transformation of matter into spirit.

The image itself may be seen as a complex bind-rune, where **Gyfu** and **Ing** are combined with **Eolh** and **Calc** (you may identify other runes as well...). This provides a contained image that is quite mandalic and could also represent the unified self. It inherently contains much of the imagery of the runes that precede it, and orders them into a unified whole. It is certainly a better alternative to the 'blank' rune suggested by some modern rune-makers to serve this psychic function.

Gar as a symbol of a spear is quite a challenge, and one that reinforces the sacrificial motif. The element air predominates in this rune, and – although a little farfetched – could the image also represent the bellows that fan (inspire) the alchemical process? A symbol of the descent of spirit into matter, maybe?

3

Sample Readings

I have made my own Futhorc. I have a selection of flat slate pieces and river stones that I use for making runes. I continually add to this collection, from various sources, and I experiment with styles of engraving and inscription, as well as making differing sets. For example, I have an Elder Futhark made from river stones sourced in central Australia and a Younger Futhark on engraved on slate. The Futhorc I am using here is also made from slate. The particular 'set' I have used for these readings was a varied process extending from the above. I have used an engraving tool to carve rune shapes into the slate, and have then used my own blood to mark and sanctify each rune in a ritual manner. The runes are kept in a pouch that is used specifically for this purpose alone.

A Rune for the Day

This method is described in the Divination section; it is the first method outlined there.

This morning I took the rune pouch and put my hand inside. I then 'felt' around the runes, sight unseen, and drew one that seemed to attract me.

It was **Ior:**

Some prior reflection: I had slept deeply following a meeting I had had the day before with my professional colleagues in Blue Fire Health, where we had discussed this book, amongst other things. As this meeting was on a Sunday it had also created a little domestic disruption, but I was also determined that what I see as my emerging more mythic direction – and my commitment to it – be primary in my life henceforth.

When I drew **Ior** the first thing that struck me was that I had chosen a rune from the runic extension, and that I had determined beforehand that this day I would write the 'Rune for the Day' with whatever rune I chose. This followed a recent discussion with one colleague about how to complete the book with these 'sample readings'.

Ior speaks to me of core or primal energy, undifferentiated and sexually androgynous. At present my sexual energy feels quite remote, yet I also felt quite strong and powerful at the time I drew the rune, so maybe this is indicating creative energy? I take the reading this way, and prepare for my day accordingly.

My understanding of the rune was that it indicated to me a confirmation of the direction I had opted for. My core energy is craving this transition, and I have been particularly entranced by the runic extension to the Futhorc and the spiritual significance in the Northumbrian runes. As this rune is, in some ways, a transition to this, it is both a confirmation and also a clear indication that some of my core interests – sexuality and gender issues – need to be the foundation and taken into this further enquiry.

A Divinatory Reading

This method is described in the Divination section and is the second method outlined there.

Being in the groove from the above reading, I now decide – as I am writing this – to do a reading to provide some clarity and an orientation of my work with both the Futhorc and the Blue Fire Health project from here, and specifically into Anglo-Saxon magic, medicine and spirituality.

I am apprehensive – even a little anxious – and find myself prevaricating... but it is time to draw the runes:

ᚱ ᚫ ᛋ

I am immediately drawn to the middle rune, **Calc**, then I look to the runes on each side – that are more familiar to me from my Elder Futhark 'days' – to gain a little of the context. Without reference to any text, I am gaining an initial impression, so I will now go to have a cup of coffee and contemplate them a little before writing further...

Further thoughts

The first rune, **Rad**, is a familiar one. In the present context it may indicate a progression from the 'daily reading' I conducted earlier in the day, but also indicates to me the beginning of the next stage with all the inferences contained in that reading. I am also drawn to the delicate balance here between my intent and the forces I am dealing with, some of which – sexuality and gender – are embedded in **Ior** as well.

Rad is leading me toward **Calc**, a rune with which I am less familiar, so I look at my own reading with more attention than usual. Again, I have drawn a rune from the runic extension, although this time from the Northumbrian extension and without a rune poem to guide me. I think this reinforces my commitment to using the Futhorc runes, but also that this rune particularly highlights the death and transition – even transformation – of the process I am presently involved in.

In terms of content, the image of the Holy Grail has interested me for many years. Over a generation ago I had considered interrupting my medical career to write a PhD thesis on the Grail. The fact I didn't do so may indicate I wasn't yet ready or mature enough; maybe I am now, and maybe it also indicates my interest to be in this transitional era, when mystical Christianity was extant and now sadly lacking in our era. Is this a task for me? A process I am destined to be involved in? I look to the last rune, as it might help me.

Eoh indicates 'strength, durability, and resilience' and 'reflects the connection to heritage and the ancestors' according to my own reading. The connection to the body and the spine particularly reminds me of the comments around kundalini energy I made about the **Ior** rune. The image of the bow may point to a more distant future that I am involved in, as represented by the yew and extending from my own ancestral heritage. Death is also symbolically present, continuing from **Calc**, so this seems to be a time of great transition for me if the outcome is not to be taken literally. Maybe I have no choice but to follow the wyrd that the runes have lain out for me.

The three runes can thus be connected. The first is where I come from, what is now behind and beneath me. I have begun and am on a journey, driven by powerful forces and with spiritual intent. The second rune tells me where I am now presently positioned. It points to my spiritual interests being the core of the challenge that faces me and with which I now have to work. The third rune is the direction I am going, the future. I will require strength and resilience, but also this is a marathon and not a sprint – maybe a legacy even beyond my own lifetime.

Collectively these runes point to challenges of my ancestry and heritage, rather than to personal issues. In the light of what preceded the question – the direction of Blue Fire Health – I would also take this reading back into that context, as it will help me define my role and direction within this collective enterprise. At a deeper level I believe it is directing me toward a clear avenue of my spiritual pursuits and their creative expression.

To reinforce this reading, the three runes could be combined into a bind-rune. To do this I take the vertical stave of each rune and superimpose them; you may also care to try doing this with pen and paper. The individual attributes are then placed around, as if the runes are stacked one on top of the other: there is a cross on the lower left hand side, with **Rad** showing clearly to the right. The resulting pictograph may capture other runes; in this case there is **Gyfu** with the cross (and maybe a Christian reinforcement), which appears to be 'supporting' **Rad** as the main thrust of the bind-rune and indicating the importance of the journey rather than the destination.

4

Postscript to Runelore

The Futhorc

My approach to the exploration of the Futhorc rune row is predominantly intuitive. Thus there is no ready reading of 'this rune means this', but a more interlaced and interlocking picture; a bit like a tapestry, I like to think. This can be seen with the frequent cross referencing to other runes, which those readers interested can readily easily extend upon, using the rune shapes and imagery as a guide.

The extension to the Futhorc contains some intriguing patterns. The initial runes 25 to 27 seem an extension of the more familiar and natural images contained in many prior runes, with the emphasis on trees that may also relate to the parallel Celtic tradition of Ogham. Sometimes referred to as the Celtic Tree Alphabet, Ogham was also present in the time period 400 CE – 1100 CE, particularly toward the western regions of the British Isles.

In simplistic terms Ogham and the connection of the Celtic priesthood – the Druids maybe – with trees is popular and remains strong. It makes sense that there would have been a cross-fertilisation process with Ogham and the emerging Futhorc, even an assimilation of the former into the latter over time and distinctive to the Futhorc, with its development from and beyond the Germanic Elder Futhark and unique to England.

It should not be forgotten that these magical systems – and the Futhorc in particular with the present study – did not arrive out of the blue, but would have emerged from earlier proto-alphabets, language, and other more symbolic means of communication in an evolving, fluid and organic process. This is suggested in various places here and I would hold it to be self-evident. It is also suggested by the linear progression of the rune row itself, where the more primitive and natural becomes increasingly more symbolic and esoteric. This could also be metaphorically seen as a temporal flow from the Neolithic through to the Middle Ages.

Neither should the Christian tradition be ignored, and it is frequently referred to above. It is tempting to try to exorcise the Christian influence in the Futhorc to 'get back to' some sort of prior pagan 'authenticity'. But I hold this to be a modern fantasy, along with other New Age aspirations; it would be better to consider the process in its reality and entirety. Because I do not consider the Christian influences to have simply usurped or suppressed the prior pagan traditions, but to have frequently and creatively merged with them, particularly if the more mystical undercurrents are explored. The cunning ('kenning') amongst the pagan magicians may well have adopted Christianity as a method in the maintenance and further development of their traditional values, as well as accepting valid spiritual 'ideas' within the new Tradition.

This trend becomes more evident after the 27th rune. Rune 28, **Ior**, has some features that I have likened to the eastern concept of kundalini. **Ear**, rune 29, is more elemental with earth and transformative with its focus on death. The image also has features that repeat in **Cweorth** (rune 30) and **Stan** (rune 32). The elemental theme is also present in these latter runes; fire, water, earth and air are all there if you scratch the surface.

You can also see below the surface some of the esoteric and symbolic imagery that extends from the elements, such as stone, spear, and chalice. The remarkable similarity here to the esoteric Christian Tradition needs reinforcing, particularly with the proto-Grail imagery; maybe foreshadowing the development of the rich corpus that would emerge over the next centuries, following the closure of the Viking age, and then with the creative emergence of the Arthurian myths in the next millennium.

I have also emphasised the alchemical themes and associations, which can be seen to connect to this trend and its development, yet also look back deep into pre-history, as do many if not all of the themes explored here.

That these latter developments occurred in northern England, which is why this sequence is referred to as Northumbrian, may not be a surprise. This region was the meeting ground of differing peoples and their influences. The Christian Church there was also suitably distant from Rome and somewhat idiosyncratic. It may not then be a surprise that it became a breeding ground for spiritual ideas that emerged in the succeeding centuries and influence us still, having deep roots in our indigenous pre-Christian spirituality.

Tradition

I have chosen a Traditional approach to the runes, but why?

There are modern versions available, such as Guido von List's attempt at the turn of the last century to unify the runes with Havamal, coming up with an 18-rune sequence. There is also Ralph Blum's attempt to accommodate a rune for the 'self' within the Elder Futhark, the argument for which was negated when we considered the **Gar** rune of the Futhorc.

Yet I have deliberately chosen to link the runes back to Tradition. My experience is that we neglect Tradition at our peril and that any attempt at modernisation should stem, with some sort of continuity, from Tradition. It is debatable where 'Tradition' starts with the runes, but we do have some basis to consider the above discussions to rest within it reasonably authentically. And, of course, it is further debatable as to how accurate this representation is, given its personal and somewhat idiosyncratic rendering.

Certainly there are modern variations in interpretation, particularly with phonetics. I am sure many of the apparent 'gaps' will be filled in over time and some of the more contentious areas clarified, although it does seem that we have a fairly exhausted corpus to draw on in the absence of any further significant discoveries. It may also be that the more we unearth, the more confusing the picture gets, leaving our desire for clarity in the realm of a modern fantasy. Some aspects, such as how exactly the Anglo-Saxons spoke, will remain forever unknown, and some further aspects will be ultimately and remain essentially unknowable.

I am not espousing Tradition in some sort of regressive manner. I just believe that it is important that any modern understanding of the runes – and other similar material from Tradition – should have some sort of continuity to remain authentic. Otherwise it is very easy to introduce subjective and personal interpretations that have only limited validity; we see all too much of this in New Age spirituality, which has also tainted the field of runology.

Yet this is all in the service of advancing Tradition into the present and future. I contend that it is the loss of Tradition that leaves us somewhat rudderless in the modern era, leaving us lacking depth, and thus living in a kind of two-dimensional scientific and technological 'flatland'. I am certainly not taking a regressive position here; I believe we connect back to Tradition, but with our feet in the present, and our vision toward the future.

This is more specifically the case when Christianity is losing its relevance in our time. When I initially began to explore the runes, I thought I would discover my pagan roots and establish a reconnection. I certainly have done that; but I have also found that there is a 'Christian theme' in the Futhorc that has embraced the more mystical spirituality of Christianity and furthered it. It is this more esoteric undercurrent that I believe has significant relevance in our time as we reach the end of the scientific era.

Other Disciplines

Here I am going to draw on what is of personal interest and where it relates to my personal and professional future. But, as I share this with you, you may find some resonance with what I am exploring.

The magical traditions have had a significant revival in modern times. But, as I have discussed in the text, I believe it is important to link this development with our heritage. I have found that runology adequately fulfils this need. The above can be extended to magical practice in the operative sense, as well as ritual and ceremony; all sadly lacking in our times, when the magical 'will' is somehow disparaged as mere 'ego'.

As a medical practitioner I am also fascinated that the Anglo-Saxon mentality did not have a 'mind-body' dualistic mentality to health, but had a more integrated vision that included the realms of superstition, magic, and the work of the spiritual. Academic inquiry has revealed that Anglo-Saxon medicine is not a mere poor cousin to Mediterranean-based medical systems and is more applicable to our mentality.

I believe these undercurrents have a lot to tell us about modern medicine and where it has gone astray by excluding this wider and spiritual dimension of 'mind', and I will be exploring these themes in more detail in the future.

Making Your Own Runes – A Reprise

Well, I did kind of leave this a little unsaid, didn't I?

Of course it is possible to make your own runes. I started with slate that I bought from my local hardware store and then progressed to river pebbles. Wood is a good medium, particularly for the magical practice of spells and curses, as the rune staves can be destroyed (sacrificed). I have used an engraving tool and coloured permanent markers for the runic symbols, but there is more... hence the title of this book: *Just Add Blood*.

Without going more deeply into the symbolism of blood, can I just say that it is a very, very powerful medium. To use it to colour the engraved runic symbols involves a ritual and symbolic 'sacrifice'. It is highly recommended, but with all the usual caveats that you see in print these days. You may just need a friendly shamanistic 'practitioner' to guide you through the process!

But where there's a 'will', there's a way.

Comparative Runology

A glance at the first appendix amends my rather restricted reference to date regarding the phonetic aspects of the runes, although the reason for this relative omission was discussed and explained earlier. In this appendix I have added the phonetic value of the 33 runes of the Futhorc to the graphic symbol of each and its name, then followed this with a similar description of both the Elder and Younger Futharks.

This addition may be useful if you have only an Elder Futhark rune row to work with, or if you choose it as a viable option. But the appendix is also designed to give an outline of the three rune rows for comparative purposes, as together these form the basis of our modern appreciation of the runic corpus.

Please do not be under the modern apprehension that this study will provide a unified picture. You may have appreciated by now that there is a considerable variation in the Futhorc and this only increases when the remaining two Futharks are considered. Instead we have a rich and varied field, with many branches and strands. Our modern appreciation in general, and mine in particular, is simply an ongoing part of this fluid process.

Instead it can be seen that each feature – symbol, name, and phonetic value (plus the meanings outlined above and in the poems) – can be explored in its own right. The symbols and names have an overall cohesion, particularly when considered over time, although some retain a consistency whilst others become much more varied.

The phonetic values connect the runes with their use as an alphabet, yet also expand this to their common usage as a script and for communication, whereas the symbols and names take on a more esoteric and magical usage. There is still a lot of disagreement regarding phonetics, and I have had to bite the bullet and chose one approach in the tables below; this is a system you may wish to modify from personal research and experience, and this is entirely valid: I contend this is a living Tradition. This philological approach is also of great value in the extended exploration of the runes beyond their magical usage.

An interesting and intriguing exercise is to explore this network of inter-relationships between the differing rune rows of the Futharks, as well as over the time period of their evolution. For example, the phonetic values give some indication of how the Elder was 'reduced' to the Younger Futhark and where omitted runes gained different associations in those retained. Additionally runes can be given differing phonetic values, particularly when the vowels are considered.

This exercise can be extended to the symbols and names, because I have taken only one theme in several possible ones here, as well as with the phonetic values. For example, many rune shapes have alternatives. In the Futhorc the **Ing** rune can have extensions upward and downwards to the left and right, as described in the text of that rune. Both **Ur** and **Sigel** can be shaped slightly differently. Similarly with the names, **Wyn** can be **Wynn**, **Sigel** can be **Sigil**, and **Hagal** can be **Haegl** as discussed. So, as well as the philological approach, an etymological study can be undertaken.

To explore all this you may need lots of paper and coloured pens, as well as access to the reference books in the index; because I have taken a fairly single and somewhat arbitrary line through these various options according to personal inclination and magical intent.

As hinted at with the phonetic values, there are wider connections that can be considered. In the Futhorc this becomes more obvious with the Northumbrian rune extension, where cultural and religious issues start to become more obvious. Also some symbols get more focus and attention, as well as others starting to look more like bind-runes than single runes.

Ultimately the runes must be considered in this wider cultural context, as well as with the cultures that preceded their clear manifestation and that continued in parallel with their influence. Remember, of course, that our modern culture is having an active influence on the appreciation of the runes and their further development into the future.

Runology remains a work in progress.

Appendix A

The Three Futharks

English Futhorc

Name	Phonetic Value	Rune
Feoh	f	ᚠ
Ur	u	ᚢ
Thorn	th	ᚦ
Os	o	ᚩ
Rad	r	ᚱ
Cen	c (k)	ᚲ
Gyfu	g	ᚷ
Wyn	w	ᚹ
Hagal	h	ᚻ
Nyd	n	ᚾ
Is	i	ᛁ
Ger	y	ᛄ
Eoh	eo	ᛇ
Peorth	p	ᛈ
Eolh	x/z	ᛉ
Sigel	s	ᛋ
Tir	t	ᛏ
Beorc	b	ᛒ
Eh	e	ᛖ
Man	m	ᛗ
Lagu	l	ᛚ
Ing	ng	◇
Ethel	e (oe)	ᛟ
Daeg	d	ᛞ
Ac	a	ᚪ
Aesc	ae	ᚫ

Yr	y	ᛣ
Ior	eo (io)	ᛡ
Ear	ea	ᛠ
Cweorth	q	ᛢ
Calc	k	ᛤ
Stan	st	ᛥ
Gar	(g)	ᚸ

Elder Futhark

Name	Phonetic Value	Rune
Fehu	f	ᚠ
Uruz	u	ᚢ
Thurisaz	th	ᚦ
Ansuz	a	ᚨ
Raido	r	ᚱ
Kenaz	k	ᚲ
Gebo	g	ᚷ
Wunjo	w	ᚹ
Hagalaz	h	ᚺ
Nauthiz	n	ᚾ
Isa	i	ᛁ
Jera	j	ᛃ
Eiwaz	i/e	ᛇ
Pertho	p	ᛈ
Algiz	z/r	ᛉ
Sowilo	s	ᛋ
Tiwaz	t	ᛏ
Berkano	b	ᛒ
Ehwaz	e	ᛖ
Mannaz	m	ᛗ
Laguz	l	ᛚ
Ingwaz	ng	ᛜ

| Othala | o | ⍂ |
| Dagaz | d | ⋈ |

Younger Futhark

Name	Phonetic Value	Rune
Fe	f	ᛓ
Ur	u/o/v	ᚾ
Thurs	th/dh	ᚦ
Ass	a	ᚡ
Reidh	r	ᚱ
Kaun	k/g/ng	ᚤ
Hagall	h	ᚻ
Naudh	n	ᛏ
Iss	i/e	ᛁ
Ar	a	ᛄ
Sol	s	ᛋ
Tyr	t/d/nd	ᛏ
Bjarkan	b/p	ᛒ
Madhr	m	ᛦ
Logr	l	ᛚ
Yr	-R	ᛉ

Appendix B

The Anglo-Saxon Rune Poem

Feoh

Wealth is a comfort to all men;
yet must every man bestow it freely,
if he wish to gain honour in the sight of the Lord.

Ur

The aurochs is proud and has great horns;
it is a very savage beast and fights with its horns;
a great ranger of the moors, it is a creature of mettle.

Thorn

The thorn is exceedingly sharp,
an evil thing for any knight to touch,
uncommonly severe on all who sit among them.

Os

The mouth is the source of all language,
a pillar of wisdom and a comfort to wise men,
a blessing and a joy to every knight.

Rad

Riding seems easy to every warrior while he is indoors
and very courageous to him who traverses the high-roads
on the back of a stout horse.

Cen

The torch is known to every living man by its pale, bright flame;
it always burns where princes sit within.

Gyfu

Generosity brings credit and honour, which support one's dignity;
it furnishes help and subsistence
to all broken men who are devoid of aught else.

Wynn

Bliss he enjoys who knows not suffering, sorrow nor anxiety,
and has prosperity and happiness and a good enough house.

Haegl

Hail is the whitest of grain;
it is whirled from the vault of heaven
and is tossed about by gusts of wind
and then it melts into water.

Nyd

Trouble is oppressive to the heart;
yet often it proves a source of help and salvation
to the children of men, to everyone who heeds it betimes.

Is

Ice is very cold and immeasurably slippery;
it glistens as clear as glass and most like to gems;
it is a floor wrought by the frost, fair to look upon.

Ger

Summer is a joy to men, when God, the holy King of Heaven,
suffers the earth to bring forth shining fruits
for rich and poor alike.

Eoh

The yew is a tree with rough bark,
hard and fast in the earth, supported by its roots,
a guardian of flame and a joy upon an estate.

Peordh

Peorth is a source of recreation and amusement to the great,
where warriors sit blithely together in the banqueting-hall.

Eolh

The Eolh-sedge is mostly to be found in a marsh;
it grows in the water and makes a ghastly wound,
covering with blood every warrior who touches it.

Sigel

The sun is ever a joy in the hopes of seafarers
when they journey away over the fishes' bath,
until the courser of the deep bears them to land.

Tir

Tiw is a guiding star; well does it keep faith with princes;
it is ever on its course over the mists of night and never fails.

Beorc

The poplar bears no fruit; yet without seed it brings forth suckers,
for it is generated from its leaves.
Splendid are its branches and gloriously adorned
its lofty crown which reaches to the skies.

Eh

The horse is a joy to princes in the presence of warriors.
A steed in the pride of its hoofs,
when rich men on horseback bandy words about it;
and it is ever a source of comfort to the restless.

Mann

The joyous man is dear to his kinsmen;
yet every man is doomed to fail his fellow,
since the Lord by his decree will commit the vile carrion to the earth.

Lagu

The ocean seems interminable to men,
if they venture on the rolling bark
and the waves of the sea terrify them
and the courser of the deep heed not its bridle.

Ing

Ing was first seen by men among the East-Danes,
till, followed by his chariot,
he departed eastwards over the waves.
So the Heardingas named the hero.

Ethel

An estate is very dear to every man,
if he can enjoy there in his house
whatever is right and proper in constant prosperity.

Dæg

Day, the glorious light of the Creator, is sent by the Lord;
it is beloved of men, a source of hope and happiness to rich and poor,
and of service to all.

Ac

The oak fattens the flesh of pigs for the children of men.
Often it traverses the gannet's bath,
and the ocean proves whether the oak keeps faith
in honourable fashion.

Æsc

The ash is exceedingly high and precious to men.
With its sturdy trunk it offers a stubborn resistance,
though attacked by many a man.

Yr

Yr is a source of joy and honour to every prince and knight;
it looks well on a horse and is a reliable equipment for a journey.

Ior

Iar is a river fish and yet it always feeds on land;
it has a fair abode encompassed by water, where it lives in happiness.

Ear

The grave is horrible to every knight,
when the corpse quickly begins to cool
and is laid in the bosom of the dark earth.
Prosperity declines, happiness passes away
and covenants are broken.

Appendix C

The Norse Rune Poem

Fe

Wealth is a source of discord among kinsmen;
the wolf lives in the forest.

Ur

Dross comes from bad iron;
the reindeer often races over the frozen snow.

Thurs

Giant causes anguish to women;
misfortune makes few men cheerful.

As

Estuary is the way of most journeys;
but a scabbard is of swords.

Reidh

Riding is said to be the worst thing for horses;
Reginn forged the finest sword.

Kaun

Ulcer is fatal to children;
death makes a corpse pale.

Hagall

Hail is the coldest of grain;
Christ created the world of old.

Naudhr

Constraint gives scant choice;
a naked man is chilled by the frost.

Isa

Ice we call the broad bridge;
the blind man must be led.

Ar

Plenty is a boon to men;
I say that Frodi was generous.

Sol

Sun is the light of the world;
I bow to the divine decree.

Tyr

Tyr is a one-handed god;
often has the smith to blow.

Bjarkan

Birch has the greenest leaves of any shrub;
Loki was fortunate in his deceit.

Madhr

Man is an augmentation of the dust;
great is the claw of the hawk.

Logr

A waterfall is a River which falls from a mountain-side;
but ornaments are of gold.

Yr

Yew is the greenest of trees in winter;
it is wont to crackle when it burns.

Appendix D

The Icelandic Rune Poem

Fé – Wealth

Source of discord among kinsmen
and fire of the sea
and path of the serpent.

Úr – Shower

Lamentation of the clouds
and ruin of the hay-harvest
and abomination of the shepherd.

Thurs – Giant

Torture of women
and cliff-dweller
and husband of a giantess.

Óss – God

Aged Gautr
and prince of Ásgardr
and lord of Vallhalla.

Reid – Riding

Joy of the horsemen
and speedy journey
and toil of the steed.

Kaun – Ulcer

Disease fatal to children
and painful spot
and abode of mortification.

Hagall – Hail

Cold grain
and shower of sleet
and sickness of serpents.

Naud – Constraint

Grief of the bond-maid
and state of oppression
and toilsome work.

Iss – Ice

Bark of rivers
and roof of the wave
and destruction of the doomed.

Ár – Plenty

Boon to men
and good summer
and thriving crops.

Sól – Sun

Shield of the clouds
and shining ray
and destroyer of ice.

Tyr

God with one hand
and leavings of the wolf
and prince of temples.

Bjarken – Birch

Leafy twig
and little tree
and fresh young shrub.

Madr – Man
Delight of man
and augmentation of the earth
and adorner of ships.

Lögr – Water
Eddying stream
and broad geysir
and land of the fish.

Yr – Yew
Bent bow
and brittle iron
and giant of the arrow.
(From *Runic and Heroic Poems* by Bruce Dickins)

Appendix E: Havamal

Odin

Wounded I hung on a wind-swept gallows
For nine long nights,
Pierced by a spear, pledged to Odhinn,
Offered, myself to myself
The wisest know not from whence spring
The roots of that ancient rood

They gave me no bread,
They gave me no mead,
I looked down;
with a loud cry
I took up runes;
from that tree I fell.

Nine lays of power
I learned from the famous Bolthor, Bestla's father:
He poured me a draught of precious mead,
Mixed with magic Odrerir.

Waxed and throve well;
Word from word gave words to me,
Deed from deed gave deeds to me,

Runes you will find, and readable staves,
Very strong staves,
Very stout staves,
Staves that Bolthor stained,
Made by mighty powers,
Graven by the prophetic god,

For the gods by Odhinn, for the elves by Dain,
By Dvalin, too, for the dwarves,
By Asvid for the hateful giants,
And some I carved myself:
Thund, before man was made, scratched them,
Who rose first, fell thereafter

Know how to cut them, know how to read them,
Know how to stain them, know how to prove them,
Know how to evoke them, know how to score them,
Know how to send them, know how to send them,

Better not to ask than to over-pledge
As a gift that demands a gift,
Better not to send than to slay too many,

The first charm I know is unknown to rulers
Or any of human kind;
Help it is named,
for help it can give in hours of sorrow and anguish.

I know a second that the sons of men
Must learn who wish to be leeches.

I know a third: in the thick of battle,
If my need be great enough,
It will blunt the edges of enemy swords,
Their weapons will make no wounds.

I know a fourth:
it will free me quickly
If foes should bind me fast
With strong chains, a chant that makes Fetters spring from the feet,
Bonds burst from the hands.

I know a fifth: no flying arrow,
Aimed to bring harm to men,
Flies too fast for my fingers to catch it
And hold it in mid-air.

I know a sixth:
it will save me if a man
Cut runes on a sapling's Roots
With intent to harm; it turns the spell;
The hater is harmed, not me.

If I see the hall
Ablaze around my bench mates,
Though hot the flames, they shall feel nothing,
If I choose to chant the spell.

I know an eighth:
that all are glad of,
Most useful to men:
If hate fester in the heart of a warrior,
It will soon calm and cure him.

I know a ninth:
when need I have
To shelter my ship on the flood,
The wind it calms, the waves it smoothes
And puts the sea to sleep,

I know a tenth:
if troublesome ghosts
Ride the rafters aloft,
I can work it so they wander astray,
Unable to find their forms,
Unable to find their homes.

I know an eleventh:
when I lead to battle Old comrades in-arms,
I have only to chant it behind my shield,
And unwounded they go to war,
Unwounded they come from war,
Unscathed wherever they are.

I know a twelfth:
If a tree bear
A man hanged in a halter,
I can carve and stain strong runes
That will cause the corpse to speak,
Reply to whatever I ask.

I know a thirteenth
if I throw a cup of water over a warrior,
He shall not fall in the fiercest battle,
Nor sink beneath the sword,

I know a fourteenth, that few know:
If I tell a troop of warriors
About the high ones, elves and gods,
I can name them one by one.
(Few can the nit-wit name.)

I know a fifteenth,
that first Thjodrerir
Sang before Delling's doors,
Giving power to gods, prowess to elves,
Fore-sight to Hroptatyr Odhinn,

I know a sixteenth:
if I see a girl
With whom it would please me to play,

I can turn her thoughts, can touch the heart
Of any white armed woman.

I know a seventeenth:
if I sing it,
the young Girl will be slow to forsake me.

I know an eighteenth that I never tell
To maiden or wife of man,
A secret I hide from all
Except the love who lies in my arms,
Or else my own sister.

To learn to sing them, Loddfafnir,
Will take you a long time,
Though helpful they are if you understand them,
Useful if you use them,
Needful if you need them.

The Wise One has spoken words in the hall,
Needful for men to know,
Unneedful for trolls to know:

Hail to the speaker,
Hail to the knower,
Joy to him who has understood,
Delight to those who have listened.

(W. H. Auden & P. B. Taylor translation)

Bibliography

General Runelore

Aswynn, Freya. *Northern Mysteries & Magick*. St. Paul, Llewellyn Publications, 2002

Fries, Jan. *Helrunar: A Handbook of Rune Magick*. Oxford, Mandrake, 2006

Thorsson, Edred. *Runelore*. York Beach, Samuel Weiser Inc. 1987

Thorsson, Edred. *Futhark: A Handbook of Rune Magic*. York Beach, Samuel Weiser Inc. 1984

Anglo-Saxon Runes

Albertsson, Alaric. *Wyrdworking: The Path of a Saxon Sorcerer*. Woodbury, Llewellyn, 2011

Bates, Brian. *The Way of Wyrd*. Carlsbad, Hay House, 2005

Elliott, RWV. *Runes: An Introduction*. Westport, Greenwood Press, 1959

Page, RI. *An Introduction to English Runes*. Woodbridge, Boydell Press, 2006

Pennick, Nigel. *Rune Magic: The History and Practice of Ancient Runic Traditions*. London, Thorsons, 1995

Tyson, Donald. *Rune Magic*. St. Paul, Llewellyn, 1995

This is but a brief outline of the runic corpus.

All the listed books are about runes, with some extension; the exception is Brian Bates' *Way of Wyrd*, which has been included because it is a brilliant portrayal of the Anglo-Saxon world and has a large bibliography.

The general books are based on the Elder Futhark and give a sound introduction with many avenues of exploration. The Futhorc Anglo-Saxon works are solely academic (Page), or with a contrasting and significantly broader appreciation and insight (Elliott), extending to the more familiar, yet differing styles of

Albertsson, Pennick, and Tyson.

These writers were also chosen as they are significant in the field, and can be used to source further material in the disciplines that suit the reader. There are many possible avenues to explore from here, but this material will provide the road maps.

Biography

Dr Kennan Taylor is a holistic physician and psychotherapist in private practice, who trained in Oxford and London universities, before emigrating to Australia. An ordained shamanic minister, member of a druid order (OBOD) and former Jungian analyst, Kennan's interests now focus on Anglo-Saxon magic, medicine, and spirituality; the challenges these present to modern life, and specifically within Australian culture. Kennan is a polymath and author with controversial views on modern medicine and the need for spiritual inclusiveness. These interests extend to counselling, teaching and mentorship in shamanic medicine, both professionally and to the online community, as expressed in Blue Fire Health.

Kennan's website is: www.bluefirehealth.com

Moon Books invites you to begin or deepen your encounter with Paganism, in all its rich, creative, flourishing forms.